The Teacher's Guide to Action Research for Special Education in PK–12 Classrooms

MARLA J. LOHMANN

Colorado Christian University

ROWMAN & LITTLEFIELD
Lanham • Boulder • New York • London

Associate Acquisitions Editor: Courtney Packard
Assistant Acquisitions Editor: Sarah Rinehart
Sales and Marketing Inquiries: textbooks@rowman.com

Credits and acknowledgments for material borrowed from other sources, and reproduced with permission, appear on the appropriate pages within the text.

Published by Rowman & Littlefield
An imprint of The Rowman & Littlefield Publishing Group, Inc.
4501 Forbes Boulevard, Suite 200, Lanham, Maryland 20706
www.rowman.com

86-90 Paul Street, London EC2A 4NE

British Library Cataloguing in Publication Information available

Library of Congress Cataloging-in-Publication Data

Names: Lohmann, Marla J., author.
Title: The teacher's guide to action research for special education in
    PK-12 classrooms / Marla J. Lohmann.
Description: Lanham, Maryland : Rowman & Littlefield, 2023. | Includes
    bibliographical references and index.
Identifiers: LCCN 2022035121 (print) | LCCN 2022035122 (ebook) | ISBN
    9781538155196 (cloth) | ISBN 9781538155202 (paperback) | ISBN
    9781538155219 (epub)
Subjects: LCSH: Special education—Research—Methodology. | Action
    research in education. | Individualized education programs.
Classification: LCC LC3969 .L59 2023 (print) | LCC LC3969 (ebook) | DDC
    371.9—dc23/eng/20220831
LC record available at https://lccn.loc.gov/2022035121
LC ebook record available at https://lccn.loc.gov/2022035122

♾️™ The paper used in this publication meets the minimum requirements of American National Standard for Information Sciences—Permanence of Paper for Printed Library Materials, ANSI/NISO Z39.48-1992.

This book is dedicated to the special education teachers who work hard every day to support the needs of children with disabilities. The world is a better place because of each of you. Thank you!

Brief Contents

Contents

List of Figures, Tables, and Textboxes

....

....

Acknowledgments

I would like to thank those who have supported me in writing this textbook. Writing a book really is a team effort and I could not have done this alone. First, I would like to thank my family for inspiring me throughout the process—thank you, Mark, Abigail, Charlotte, Esther, and Abraham. I love you all and am so thankful for the countless ways you support me every day! I would like to thank my colleagues who encouraged me to keep writing and reminded me why we need this book in our own teacher preparation classrooms. Thank you to Drs. Kathleen Hogan, Ruby Owiny, and Jennifer Walker. Finally, thank you to the folks at Rowman & Littlefield who gave me the opportunity and support I needed to make this textbook a reality. Thank you, Mark Kerr and Courtney Packard.

What Is Special Education Action Research?

....

Student Learning Objectives

After reading chapter 1 and completing the exercises at the end of the chapter, students will be able to:

- Identify the purpose of action research.
- Describe ways that they use data and informal action research to make decisions in their daily lives.
- Compare and contrast action research and traditional research in the field of special education.
- Summarize the benefits to using action research in the special education classroom.
- Identify school-based issues and categorize them based on whether they should be addressed through traditional research or action research.

Mr. Bullock is an elementary self-contained special education teacher who is currently pursuing his master's degree in special education. He teaches a classroom full of students with a variety of needs and abilities, including two kindergarteners with severe autism, a third, fourth, and sixth grader who have each been diagnosed as having an intellectual disability, and second-grade twin brothers who qualify for special education services due to emotional disabilities. As Mr. Bullock is nearing the end of his master's degree program, he has been asked to complete an action research project to demonstrate his learning; he is considering projects that he can complete to meet that requirement while supporting the needs of the students in his classroom.

....

L ike Mr. Bullock, you may be preparing to complete an action research project—sometimes also referred to as practitioner research—that addresses learning or behavior needs for a student with a disability. In fact, I would venture to guess that you are reading this book because you are currently taking a course on action research or data-based decision making in the special education classroom. Action research is a valuable tool that we can use to aid us in making decisions, both large and small. I suspect that when you heard the word "research," some of you felt a bit of panic; I want to assure you that action research is not hard nor scary. In fact, you conduct small-scale action research projects multiple times a day without even realizing it and without considering your actions as research. Every time you use data and information to make a decision, you are conducting informal action research.

WHAT IS RESEARCH?

Before we start to talk about action research, though, it is important to understand the term "research" and what it means. When they hear the word "research," many people think of rats running mazes in a lab while people in white coats and goggles watch them and make notes on their clipboards. This is one form of research, but in reality, most research does not look like this. Most research does not involve mice nor lab coats nor goggles. You may use a clipboard for data collection, and you will certainly be making observations and testing theories, but you most likely will not look like the typical image of a scientist as you conduct action research in your classroom.

Research is a systematic process used to better understand a phenomena or situation through the collection and analysis of data (Ravid, 2020). When we conduct research, we make a hypothesis, or educated guess, about a problem and then use a systematic process to test that hypothesis (Ary et al., 2018). As a student, you likely learned about the scientific process, which includes six steps:

1. Observing a problem or phenomena that the researcher would like to better understand
2. Collecting initial (or baseline) data about the problem
3. Considering potential explanations for the situation and forming a hypothesis
4. Designing an experiment, or series of experiments, to test that hypothesis
5. Carrying out the experiment and analyzing the results
6. Sharing the new knowledge or form a new hypothesis if the experiment results did not support the hypothesis (Voit, 2019)

These same six steps are used in almost all research studies. So, as you consider using action research, think back to your experiences in high school science class. Use the skills you learned then to support you as a teacher today.

ACTION RESEARCH IN DAILY LIFE

When we consider the scientific method, I want you to consider how frequently you use data and inquiry (essentially action research) to make decisions in your daily life. Personally, I use it a lot! This week, I have used the concepts of action research to test out a variety of ideas and make decisions. This paragraph offers a few examples of how the concept of action research is used in my day-to-day life. I use action research methods in the kitchen; yesterday, I baked muffins and doubled the amount of cinnamon called for in the recipe. I was testing my hypothesis that more cinnamon would make the muffins taste better. My hypothesis was correct, and I will continue putting extra cinnamon in my muffins! I use action research methods in my quest to get healthy; I am currently training to run a half-marathon and have been tracking the distance I run each day and my speed, as well as when I take rest days. Based on what I have read from professional athletes, low-intensity exercise days are better for some runners than are complete rest days; so far, my data supports this concept for me. I also use action research when I interact with my children. Earlier this week, my sixth-grade daughter sat at her desk, crying while she tried to do her homework. She is not typically an emotional child, so I hypothesized that she might be sick. My suspicion was confirmed when I took her temperature. Like me, I suspect that you can think of many ways that you use data and information to make decisions throughout the day, in both your personal and professional life. In its simplest form, this use of data (whether numerical, observational, or other data) is action research.

THE ACTION RESEARCH PROCESS

Action research is the process of (a) identifying a problem or challenge, (b) collecting data to better understand the problem, (c) researching evidence-based interventions for addressing the problem, (d) selecting and implementing an intervention, (e) collecting data to determine the effectiveness of the intervention, and (f) making changes to the intervention based on that data. In the special education classroom, action research in the form of data-based decision-making is an integral part of the IEP (Individualized Education Program) process and should be used in IEP planning, implementation, and evaluation. Figure 1.1 offers a visual representation of this process.

```
┌─────────────────────────────────────────────────────────────┐
│                    Identify a problem                        │
│                           ⇩                                  │
│                  Collect baseline data                       │
│                           ⇩                                  │
│            Research evidence-based intervention              │
│                           ⇩                                  │
│         Select and implement an appropriate intervention     │
│                           ⇩                                  │
│    Collect data to determine the effectiveness of the intervention │
│                           ⇩                                  │
│     Make adjustments to intervention plan to meet student needs │
└─────────────────────────────────────────────────────────────┘
```

FIGURE 1.1. Flowchart of Special Education Action Research Process

ACTION RESEARCH IN THE IEP PROCESS

For special educators, action research is a process that should be used on an ongoing basis to support the unique needs of the learners in our classroom. Action research is a critical practice for special education teachers for two primary reasons: the use of evidence-based instruction is mandated by federal law and the research tells us that classroom instruction and individual interventions are more effective when we make data-based decisions (Poortman & Schildkamp, 2016).

We are mandated to follow the guidelines outlined in the Individuals with Disabilities Education Act (IDEA) and the Every Student Succeeds Act (ESSA), which both indicate that teachers must use evidence-based instructional practices, based on peer-reviewed research, when supporting students with disabilities. (The exact verbiage from both laws can be found in table 1.1.)

These legal mandates for the use of data to make educational decisions are based on the research supporting the benefits. Step three of the action research process (researching evidence-based interventions for addressing the problem) ensures that teachers look for evidence-based practices when designing interventions for students with disabilities. An evidence-based practice is a teaching strategy, method, or intervention that has proven to be effective through rigorous, peer-reviewed research methods (Cook et al., 2008). As classroom teachers, we can select evidence-based interventions to implement in our classrooms and

TABLE 1.1. ESSA and IDEA verbiage related to evidence-based instruction

ESSA Section 8101(21)(A)	"(21) EVIDENCE-BASED.— (A) IN GENERAL.— Except as provided in subparagraph (B), the term 'evidence-based,' when used with respect to a State, local educational agency, or school activity, means an activity, strategy, or intervention that— (i) demonstrates a statistically significant effect on improving student outcomes or other relevant outcomes based on— (I) strong evidence from at least 1 well-designed and well-implemented experimental study; (II) moderate evidence from at least 1 well-designed and well-implemented quasi-experimental study; or (III) promising evidence from at least 1 well designed and well-implemented correlational study with statistical controls for selection bias; or (ii)(I) demonstrates a rationale based on high quality research findings or positive evaluation that such activity, strategy, or intervention is likely to improve student outcomes or other relevant outcomes; and (II) 11 includes ongoing efforts to examine the effects of such activity, strategy, or intervention."
Describes the varying categories of evidence-based practices that may be used to support students, including students receiving special education services	
IDEA Section 1414(d)(1)(A)(i) (IV)	"a statement of the special education and related services and supplementary aids and services, **based on peer-reviewed research** to the extent practicable, to be provided to the child, or on behalf of the child, and a statement of the program modifications or supports for school personnel that will be provided for the child—"
Discusses what must be included in every students' Individualized Education Program (IEP)	

use the action research process to determine if the selected interventions are appropriate for meeting the needs of the individual students we teach.

When we conduct action research, we formulate our study based on evidence-based interventions and use data to determine the appropriateness of that intervention for our specific classroom. Special education teachers understand that data collection is important for supporting the needs of children with disabilities (Ruble et al., 2018), but teachers are often inconsistent at using this process for supporting learners (Wayman et al., 2012). In fact, only one-third of teachers use the data they have collected to make educational decisions for students with disabilities (Brawley & Stormont, 2014). Reading this book will help you know how to use the data you are collecting and will, hopefully, encourage you to make data-driven decisions for supporting the needs of all learners in your classroom.

It should be noted, though, that teachers must be careful regarding how they use the data they collect. We must collect data to understand children's needs and improve instruction and ensure that we are not designing instructional activities and assessments that lead to the data results we want to find and report (Kim, 2016). The data we collect must inform and improve our teaching, and accurate data analysis is important, which means some teachers may need assistance in interpreting the data (Wohlstetter et al., 2008). This book attempts to guide you in understanding how to interpret and use the data you are collecting in your classroom so that you can best meet the needs of your students.

TRADITIONAL RESEARCH VERSUS ACTION RESEARCH

As you begin to think about action research, it is important that you understand the differences between action research and traditional research. Both forms of research are critical for ensuring high quality instruction and interventions for students with disabilities, but they are different in both purpose and implementation.

Traditional education research is designed to investigate a specific question or test a theory related to instruction or schools but may not have immediate application in a classroom (Tuckman & Harper, 2012). Traditional research studies are planned and conducted by researchers, who are often university faculty members and are outside the community being studied. Teachers follow the protocol provided to them by the researchers in implementing any interventions, but they do not themselves design the interventions nor analyze the data (Hughes, 2003).

Action research in the special education classroom involves teachers using their personal knowledge and experience to guide the research. The research is conducted within their own classrooms and schools and is designed to address a specific concern or need at the time. Action research is conducted as a way for teachers to use reflective practices and structured inquiry to address issues and challenges in their own classrooms (Manfra, 2009). Action research is used to make changes that support students in the classroom (Johnston, 2005). This change is based on teacher reflection on the data that is collected (Manfra, 2009) and the changes generally occur immediately after the conclusion of the research (Cochran-Smith & Lytle, 1999). At the conclusion of action research, teachers should share what they learned with colleagues, but it is critical to understand that the results may not be generalizable to other students or classrooms (Glanz, 1999). Table 1.2 illustrates the differences and similarities of traditional and action research.

When considering both types of research, it is important to understand the need for each one and how traditional research and action research work

TABLE 1.2. Traditional research and action research similarities and differences

Traditional research	Action research
Researchers (often university faculty) are decision makers	Teachers are decision makers
Teachers often implement interventions with guidance from researchers	Teacher-researchers implement intervention
Requires data analysis and synthesis of information	Requires reflection from the teacher-researcher
Explores a theory or attempts to find a solution to a common need in schools	Solves a current need in the classroom/school
Involves multiple students, classrooms, or schools or multiple similar research studies are conducted to understand the topic	Involves one student, classroom, or school
Results should be shared with the education community	Results should be shared with colleagues
Results on a single research study (or a combination of similar research studies) may be generalized to other students and schools	Results may not be generalizable
Used to lead to change in many classrooms or schools	Used to lead to change in one classroom or school

TABLE 1.3. Which form of research is appropriate?

Traditional research	Action research
A school district wants to purchase a reading intervention program to support all struggling first-grade readers districtwide	Jafari is a first-grade student who is an English-language learner and receives special education services under the category of OHI due to his medical diagnosis of attention-deficit/hyperactivity disorder (ADHD). He has tested below grade level for phonemic awareness. His teacher wants to find an intervention that is best suited for his unique needs
A state has recently changed teacher certification requirements and now requires all new teachers to be certified to teach culturally and linguistically diverse learners, in addition to being certified in their content area. The state wants to evaluate the impact of the new teacher certification requirements on teacher quality and retention.	Mr. Phiri is the principal of a school in a largely Hispanic community. Based on feedback from parents, he believes that the teachers in his school do not understand the community culture. He wants to find a way to help the teachers learn more about their community and best practices in teaching Hispanic students.

together to support the learning of all students. As a classroom teacher, you will look at traditional research to help you find evidence-based ideas for supporting your students and will use action research to determine if those specific strategies are appropriate for your student and your classroom. Table 1.3 offers examples of school-based questions and the research format that would be appropriate for finding the answer. You will notice that traditional research questions tend to be large-scale, while action research seeks to find the answer to small-scale problems that have an impact on one student, one teacher, or one classroom.

QUANTITATIVE RESEARCH, QUALITATIVE RESEARCH, AND MIXED METHODS RESEARCH

When designing a research study, either action research or traditional research, there are various formats a research study may take. Because action research is specific to a student or classroom, it is less important that you fully understand these methods, but it is still valuable to know the distinctions, which are briefly described here.

Often, when people think of the term "research," they are thinking about data sets and analyzing large amounts of numbers, or in other words, quantitative research. Quantitative research is focused on manipulating variables and using a tool, such as a survey, to learn about a topic (Brannen, 2017). Quantitative-research methods are often considered to be more technical and freer from researcher bias; traditionally, quantitative-research study reports have been written in a neutral and impersonal tone (Tashakkori & Teddlie, 1998). In order to help me remember the meaning of quantitative research, I think about the word "quantity," which indicates numbers. In its simplest explanation, quantitative research is about numbers. In order for quantitative research results to be used to make decisions about a group of people, the number of people being studied—known as the sample size—is an important consideration, as too few study participants may lead to inaccurate or unreliable results (Martinez-Mesa et al., 2014).

Alternatively, sometimes researchers want to explore a topic in its currently existing reality and explain an existing phenomenon; in this case, they would use qualitative research methods (Brannen, 2017). Qualitative research has traditionally been conducted when the researcher has personal feelings or opinions about the topic being studied and is often reported on using informal terms and thorough narratives and descriptions (Johnson & Onwuegbuzie, 2004). For qualitative research studies, the sample size varies; qualitative research can involve just one study participant or may involve many (Boddy, 2016). Qualitative research may involve tools such as focus groups, interviews, observations, and work samples.

While both quantitative and qualitative methods are beneficial in answering many research questions, sometimes one research method is not enough. In these cases, we use a mixed-methods approach, which involves incorporating components of both quantitative and qualitative research methods into our research study design. Using a mixed-methods approach may help researchers to gain a fuller understanding of the topic being studied (Johnson & Onwuegbuzie, 2004). In order to help you better understand these three methods for designing and conducting research, table 1.4 offers examples of education research for each of the methods.

WHY SHOULD I DO ACTION RESEARCH?

You now have a basic understanding of the concept of action research, but you may still be wondering why you should use it in your classroom. Here is my simple answer: action research makes you a more effective teacher because it provides you with the knowledge and tools to support the needs of all your students. Action research is a critical practice that should occur in all classrooms. But don't take my word for it—listen to what special education teachers have to say about action research (textbox 1.1)!

TEXTBOX 1.1
WHAT TEACHERS SAY ABOUT ACTION RESEARCH

"Using the action research process helped me to address some aggressive behaviors from one student in my classroom. Now that we have those behaviors better under control, I can focus more on teaching and the children in the classroom feel safe."

—Melissa, middle school self-contained special education teacher

"Collecting data on the reading fluency of my students helped me to better understand their needs and design appropriate instruction for my class. The ongoing data collection within the action research process means that I am constantly adjusting my instruction to ensure that students are learning."

—Jose, second-grade inclusion teacher

"I designed my action research project to focus on one of my students who was frequently tardy to class. I learned that my student needed more support in planning her passing period times and organizing her class materials within her locker. Now that we have implemented individual interventions for these issues, she is rarely late to class!"

—Becca, high school special education case manager

TABLE 1.4. Research studies and the methods used

Quantitative research	Qualitative research	Mixed-methods research
A state wants to know if eighth graders are reading, and comprehending what they read, at grade level. They look at the state annual standardized test scores for all eighth-grade students over a period of five years. The state determines that 75% of eighth graders in the state are meeting the state academic standards in reading.	An eighth-grade teacher wants to know to what extent her students are comprehending the current literature unit, *The Giver*. In order to study this, she asks each student to write a paper summarizing the book and connecting it to events in their own lives. After reading the papers (work samples), the teacher determines that the majority of her students can summarize the book but cannot make connections between the reading and their own lives.	After looking at the work samples, the eighth-grade teacher believes that she has an incomplete picture of student comprehension of *The Giver*, so she creates a multiple-choice test about the book. Using student test answers and the papers, she gets a better understanding of their comprehension of *The Giver*.
Lincoln Elementary School wants to understand the behavior challenges that are occurring in their school. In order to do this, they look at all office referrals for the past two years and categorize them based on the reasons the students were referred to the office. They find that "inappropriate language" was the most-reported reason for office referrals for students in third through sixth grades and that students in kindergarten to second grade were most likely to be sent to the office for "disrespecting the teacher."	A sixth-grade teacher has noticed that the students in her classroom are using words that she considers to be inappropriate. He decides to gain a better understanding of when and how the students are using the words by collecting data in his classroom. He notes which students said the inappropriate words, what words were said, and what happened immediately before and after the event. By looking at the data, the teacher notices that most of the inappropriate words are said by two students during independent work time and that the other students tend to laugh when the inappropriate words are said.	Stoneybrook High School has seen a drastic increase in the number of student suspensions over the past few years. A new principal has just come to the school and would like to understand the reasons for the increased suspension rate. During the first semester of the school year, she keeps track of all suspensions and categorizes them by the reason for the suspension and which administrator or teacher initiated the suspension. In addition, when a student is suspended, she holds individual conferences with the student and the school faculty member to learn about the event that caused the suspension. At the end of the first

The Special Education department in Winter Valley School District is seeking to build collaborative relationships with parents/caregivers of children with disabilities. They create a survey and send it to all parents of special education students via email. The survey asks about specific ways that families choose to be involved with their children's education, caregivers' levels of satisfaction with the school, and ways that parents would like to get involved. About 20% of the parents who received the survey responded and Winter Valley School District used the data from those responses to develop systems to better partner with parents/caregivers.

Mr. Sanchez is a teacher in Summer Ridge Elementary School. He feels that he has strong collaborative working relationships with the families of most of his students, but he has noticed that there are a few families with whom he rarely communicates. These families are part of a small community that recently immigrated from Somalia. Mr. Sanchez decided to hold a focus group at the Somali community center and invite the parents to talk to him. After the focus group, Mr. Sanchez feels that he knows what the caregivers of his students need from him.

semester, she analyzes both the numerical data and the interview data. After looking at the data, she notices that the majority of the suspensions appear to result due to student-teacher conflicts.

After the Winter Valley School District parent/caregiver survey is complete, the principal of Spring Hill Middle School wants to know more about how to collaborate with the parents/caregivers of the students in her school. To learn more, she holds five online focus groups to discuss home-school collaboration. Specifically, she asks about the challenges families face in working with the school and what Spring Hill Middle School can do better to team with parents. Using the data from the districtwide survey and the themes that emerged in the focus groups, the principal formulates a plan to better collaborate with the families of children with disabilities in her school.

CONCLUSION

It is important to understand that you should be using action research to make small-scale decisions for your classroom and your students. Be cautious as you enter this process that you do not use your action research to make large-scale decisions about other students. Your action research can (and should) be used to guide the formation of other action research projects, both in your classroom and in your colleagues' classrooms. But the results of your action research alone are not sufficient to make decisions that impact many students. Don't adopt a new schoolwide curriculum or implement a new teaching method for all fifth graders based solely on the results of one action research project.

After reading this chapter, I hope you have a clearer understanding of action research and its application in the special education classroom. The beginning of this chapter opened with a short vignette about Mr. Bullock; you will find his story continuing in each of the following chapters so that you can see how one teacher might use action research to support students. Additionally, at the end of the book, you will find three case studies of action research projects. These studies and the vignettes are designed to support you in understanding how you can use action research to support a variety of learners in your classroom and school. As you read the case studies, you will likely notice that the basic process of action research is the same regardless of the student need, grade level, or teacher experience.

REVIEW QUESTIONS AND EXERCISES

1. In this chapter, you learned about the basics of action research. Based on what you have learned, consider what an action researcher might look like. Create a visual representation (drawing, computer-based image, cartoon, sculpture, etc.) of a teacher action researcher. How does this image differ from what most people think of when they hear the term "researcher." Why is it important that we broaden this traditional image of who is a researcher?

2. As noted in this chapter, we use data and the action research process to make decisions in our lives on a daily basis. List five ways you have used action research recently.

3. Create a visual representation of the action research process. Make sure that you put the steps into your own words and that your visual representation looks different from figure 1.1.

4. Think about your classroom or school (or a classroom/school where you were a student or teacher). Make a list of at least five action research topics that might be appropriate for the students in that setting.

5. In a method of your choosing (e.g., one-page paper, 3–5-minute video, or visual representation), explain what you hope to learn about action research. Consider how the action research process may benefit you as a teacher and what impact your involvement in action research will have on your students.

Identifying Classroom Learning Challenges and Collecting Baseline Data

··

Student Learning Objectives

After reading chapter 2 and completing the exercises at the end of the chapter, students will be able to do the following:

- Collect baseline data
- Use the baseline data to develop a problem statement
- Articulate a rationale for why a specific problem needs to be addressed
- Write a definition for a learning or behavior challenge

Mr. Bullock has been thinking about the action research project that he is required to do for his course and is pondering potential projects that will support the current needs of his classroom. He has several ideas, but he has decided that his most pressing need is to find a way to support Billy, one of the second-grade twin brothers. Billy has been identified as having an emotional disturbance, which manifests itself through aggressive behaviors, including self-injury and physically attacking peers. Recently, Billy has begun kicking his brother when he is frustrated and, last week, Billy kicked his brother hard enough to break the tibia in his left leg. Mr. Bullock feels that he needs to find a solution as soon as possible, so he has decided to take the opportunity to design his action research project around Billy's kicking his brother.

Y ou first encountered Mr. Bullock in chapter 1, where you read that he is a self-contained teacher who is currently completing his master's degree in special education and needs to identify an action research project. In order to identify a potential project, Mr. Bullock considered the needs of the students in his classroom and selected the student need

··

TABLE 2.1. Student needs

Student	Need	Important information	Level of urgency
Jose is a kindergartener identified with autism	Communication	Jose's IEP team recently determined that he needed some form of AAC in order to access the curriculum and he was introduced to PECS about a month ago but is not using it consistently.	High because communication is important for accessing the curriculum and for having needs met
Penelope is a kindergartener identified with autism	Screaming when school bell rings	Penelope appears to be sensitive to loud noises. Each day, when the school bell rings to begin and end the day, Penelope screams and holds her ears. This behavior can last for up to 15 minutes some days.	High due to the fact that Penelope is clearly bothered by the noise. In addition, some days the screaming is loud enough to inhibit learning in the classroom next door.
Billy is a second grader identified with an emotional disturbance	Physical aggression toward others	Billy kicks his brother and recently broke his brother's leg while kicking. Over the past month, he has also left a bruise on his brother's body almost every day.	***Critical due to potential for physical harm
Matthew is a second grader identified with an emotional disturbance	Emotional response/crying	Matthew cries when he is frustrated or overwhelmed. Challenges that are small to other students (such as missing one problem on a math assignment) can lead to him crying for 10+ minutes.	High due to the fact that the crying takes time away from Matthew's learning and prevents Matthew from learning from his mistakes on schoolwork.

DeShawn is a third grader identified with an intellectual disability	Reading fluency	DeShawn is currently reading at an early first-grade reading level, based on his testing scores for both fluency and comprehension.	High because reading is a vital skill for accessing content in all subject areas. In addition, DeShawn is self-conscious about his own reading because his younger sister can read more fluently than he can.
Avni is a fourth grader identified with an intellectual disability	Self-care/Toileting	Avni is inconsistent with toileting use and has an accident about three times each week. On some days, she wears Pull-Ups, but does not do this every day. On the days that she has an accident and is not wearing a Pull-Up, the staff must deep clean the carpet and any learning materials in the vicinity.	High due to the fact that urine on the classroom floor can be considered a hygiene issue. In addition, there are social implications to toileting accidents.
Aliyah is a sixth grader identified with an intellectual disability	Assistive technology for writing	Aliyah's IEP team has set a few goals in the area of writing and has determined that Aliyah requires assistive technology (AT) to master the writing goals. However, Mr. Bullock has not yet identified the appropriate AT for Aliyah and would like to trail several options to see which is most appropriate	High because Aliyah needs an appropriate AT tool in order to master her IEP goals in writing.

Key: AAC = augmentative and alternative communication; IEP = Individualized Education Program; PECS = Picture Exchange Communication System

that is the most critical at this time. As you consider potential action research projects, I urge you to do the same. Make a list of every concern that you have about students' academic, social-emotional, or behavioral needs. Then, identify the urgency of each need and select the most urgent need to address first. Keep in mind that any concern regarding a child's safety is critical and should be considered urgent. Table 2.1 offers an example of such a list for Mr. Bullock. Mr. Bullock chose just one need for each student in his classroom to include in this list, but you can choose to list every need you see in your own classroom. Because Mr. Bullock only listed one concern for each student, he has categorized them all as high, but if you list several concerns for the students, you may consider additional levels of urgency such as "medium" and "low."

DATA-DRIVEN DECISION-MAKING

Teachers make countless decisions every single day; some decisions are made in advance while planning classroom instruction, while other decisions happen in the spur-of-the moment as needs and situations arise (Borko et al., 2008). All decisions that teachers make are based, at least to some extent, on their own previous experiences, knowledge, opinions, and beliefs (Shavelson & Stern, 1981). While it is important to incorporate previous experience in decision making, teachers must not use their own experiences as the basis for classroom decisions. As the quote at the beginning of the chapter indicates, data is critical in making informed decisions. When you make educational decisions without data, you are basing those decisions on your opinion, which may or may not be accurate.

The ability to use data to make decisions in the classroom or school is referred to as data literacy (Mandinach & Gummer, 2013). When teachers and schools use both informal data and standardized test data to guide decisions, student outcomes are improved (Carlson et al., 2011). Using data to help you make decisions in your classroom will make you a more effective teacher and will help you achieve the goals you have set for yourself and for your students.

For special educators, data-driven decision-making is a critical component of several high-leverage practices (HLPs). The acronym HLP is used to identify research-based practices that support the needs of students with disabilities; special educators should use the HLPs to guide their work. Each of the HLPs require teachers to use data to make decisions, but several explicitly note the use of data-driven decision-making. Specifically, data is mentioned in either the title or description of the following HLPs: 4, 5, 6, 10, 11. However, each of the other HLPs implies the use of data for implementation (McLeskey et al., 2017). Textbox 2.1 provides a list of the HLPs that explicitly mention data, but the use of data to make decisions in the special education classroom is implied in many of the other HLPs.

Even though the research shows the benefit of using data to make decisions, and the fact that it is mandated under both ESSA and IDEA and is considered a special education HLP, teachers are often reluctant to use data to guide instruction in their classrooms (Brown et al., 2011) and may feel unprepared for data-driven decision-making (Borko et al., 2008; Dunn et al., 2020). In many cases, teachers "go through the motions" of collecting data and may believe they use that data for the decisions they make, but do not actually do so; in some cases, teachers even try to hinder the implementation of data-driven decision-making in their schools (Dunn, 2016). This book is designed to help you feel more comfortable in data-based decision making so that you can ensure success for all students in your classroom.

DEFINING LEARNING OR BEHAVIOR CHALLENGE

Before a teacher can begin to engage in data-based decision-making, it is vital they use an accurate definition of the learning or behavior challenge. This definition should be specific so that others know exactly what is being targeted through the action research and data collection can be consistent, even when collected by multiple stakeholders (Fox & Gable, 2004). When a teacher creates a definition of a target-learning or behavior challenge for action research, the definition must succinctly describe the problem in a manner that is clearly stated so that any other stakeholder, such as other teachers in the school and parents, understand the problem. The definition does not need to be a complete sentence but can instead simply be a short phrase that includes the name of the student and the targeted learning or behavior skill. Table 2.2

TABLE 2.2. Examples and nonexamples of definitions

Examples	Nonexamples
Johnny kicks the table and screams	Johnny throws a tantrum
Suzie tells the teacher "no" when asked to complete a nonpreferred task	Suzie misbehaves
Rafael reads at a DRA level of 10	Rafael reads below grade level
Anya yells out the answer when the teacher asks a question	Anya is disruptive
Aarush writes incomplete sentences and frequently does not use capitalization nor punctuation when he writes	Aarush is a bad writer
Xia frequently turns in work late and does not use her planner to keep track of homework and other school requirements	Xia is unorganized

Key: DRA = Developmental Reading Assessment

offers examples and nonexamples of definitions that a teacher might use in action research.

COLLECTING BASELINE DATA

Once we have defined the target behavior or skill, we can begin the data-based, decision-making process. In order to make decisions based on data, we first must have some data. The initial data we collect is referred to as baseline data. Baseline data provides us with a starting point and is used to set goals for where we want to go (Scheithauer et al., 2020). Without this initial data, we have no way to know for sure if our intervention is working. As we take data throughout our intervention, we will compare it to the baseline data to ensure that we are seeing a trend we want to see (Centers for Disease Control, 2014). Keep in mind that, while we are discussing this data-based, decision-making process as it applies to special education classrooms, the same process is used in other types of classrooms and in many other noneducation fields.

Depending on the specific skill or behavior that we are targeting, we may take data in a variety of ways. However, it is best practice to use more than one form of data collection in order to get a more complete picture of the student's baseline level; this practice is referred to as triangulation (Ravid, 2020). For an action research project, we might use data from assessments, work samples, observations, interviews, surveys, checklists, or rating scales (Efron & Ravid, 2013). In the following sections, each of these forms of data collection will be briefly presented, but I recommend learning more before you use any form of data collection.

ASSESSMENT DATA

As teachers, we assess student learning on a daily basis. Many purchased curriculums come with quizzes and tests that provide us with a snapshot of students' mastery of a set of content-related skills. In addition, many schools use curriculum-based measurements (CBMs), which are norm-referenced assessments given at regular intervals to track student progress on a specific skill such as reading fluency or math fact accuracy (Fuchs, 2004). Assessments such as CBMs and tests can be used to identify learners who may be struggling with the content by comparing students' scores with those of peers (Deno et al., 2001). In addition, curriculum-based measurements are great ways to track progress as each CBM is comparable to all the others in terms of complexity and skill level tested (January et al., 2019). Table 2.3 offers examples of commonly used CBMs that teachers may be able to access within their schools or may already be using on a regular basis. While tests and CBMs can be fantastic screening tools, keep in mind that you need to triangulate your data and that you should also be using one of the other forms of data discussed below when determining whether a student is struggling with a content skill.

WORK SAMPLES

A second option for baseline data is the use of work samples, which includes any work the student has completed either in the classroom or for homework (keeping in mind that home environments and assistance from parents or siblings may have an impact on the quality of homework submitted). Students complete and submit numerous work samples every single day. Some of these are small, like worksheets and exit tickets, while others are larger submissions, such as unit projects or presentations. But regardless of the size of the work sample, these submissions can be valuable forms of data to help teachers better understand students' learning needs. Small assignments, like worksheets or

TABLE 2.3. Commonly used curriculum-based measurements (CBM)

CBMs for reading	CBMs for Math
• Acadience Reading	• Acadience Math
• AimsWeb	• AimsWeb
• DIBELS 8th edition	• easyCBM Math
• easyCBM Reading	• STEEP
• FastBridge	

TABLE 2.4. Rubric for CCSS.ELA-LITERACY.W.7.1

Write arguments to support claims with clear reasons and relevant evidence.

Criteria	Advanced 4 points	Proficient 3 points	Learning in-progress 2 points	Novice 1 point
Introduce claim(s), acknowledge alternate or opposing claims, and organize the reasons and evidence logically.	Student presents claim with a thorough explanation of their belief. In addition, the student thoroughly presents all opposing claims. Evidence for both sides of the debate is presented in an organized and logical manner.	Student presents claim with an explanation of their belief. In addition, the student presents at least one opposing claim. Evidence for both sides of the debate is presented in an organized and logical manner.	Student presents claim but may not offer an explanation of their belief or the explanation may not be appropriate. The student presents at least one opposing claim but may not offer evidence for that claim. Evidence may not be presented in an organized and logical manner.	Student demonstrates a lack of understanding of the topic being presented or an inability to articulate their claim or the evidence.
Support claim(s) with logical reasoning and relevant evidence, using accurate, credible sources and demonstrating an understanding of the topic or text.	Student supports their claim with appropriate evidence that provides a strong case for their claim. The student uses a variety of references that are considered credible on the topic. A minimum of five references are used.	Student supports their claim with appropriate evidence that provides a strong case for their claim. The student uses references that are considered credible on the topic. A minimum of three references are used.	Student supports their claim with appropriate evidence. The student uses references that are considered credible on the topic. A minimum of one reference is used.	Student demonstrates a lack of understanding of the topic being presented and does not support their claim with evidence from credible sources.

Use words, phrases, and clauses to create cohesion and clarify the relationships among claim(s), reasons, and evidence.	The student uses clear writing that makes appropriate connections between the evidence and clarifies any discrepancies that might be presented in the evidence. Connections are made between the evidence support the student's claim as well as the evidence presenting opposing claims. The student uses transitions and clauses that are appropriate. The paper reads smoothly and is easily understood by the reader.	The student uses clear writing that makes appropriate connections between the evidence. The student uses transitions and clauses that are appropriate. The paper reads smoothly and is easily understood by the reader.	The student's writing is mostly understandable to the reader. The student makes connections between some of the evidence, but some connections are not stated in the paper. Appropriate transitions and clauses are used in some paragraphs, but not consistently throughout the paper. The paper may not read smoothly.	The student's writing is not easily understood by the reader. The student does not make connections between the evidence. Appropriate transitions and clauses may not be used.
Establish and maintain a formal style.	The student's paper is professionally written and follows the writing style as outlined by the teacher expectations. Appropriate font and font size, page numbering, title page, and citation format are used. The paper requires minimal or no editing for grammatical, spelling, and formatting errors.	The student's paper is professionally written but may include a few informal statements. The paper follows the writing styles as outlined by the teacher expectations. Appropriate font and font size, page numbering, title page, and citation format are used. The paper requires some editing for grammatical, spelling, and formatting errors.	The student's paper may be written in an informal manner and may not follow the writing style as outlined by the teacher expectations. The paper requires significant editing for grammar, spelling, and formatting errors.	The student's paper is both informally written and does not follow the writing style as outlined by the teacher expectations. The paper requires significant editing for grammar, spelling, and formatting errors.

(continued)

TABLE 2.4. (continued)

Criteria	Advanced 4 points	Proficient 3 points	Learning in-progress 2 points	Novice 1 point
Provide a concluding statement or section that follows from and supports the argument presented.	The student's paper includes a concluding section that summarizes the main points presented in the paper, including the main points that support the student's claim and the opposing claims. The conclusion includes a thesis statement that reiterates the student's claim.	The student's paper includes a concluding section that summarizes the main points presented in the paper that support the student's claim. The conclusion includes a thesis statement that reiterates the student's claim.	The student's paper includes a concluding statement that reiterates the student's claim but does not summarize the main points from the paper.	The student's paper does not include a concluding statement, or the concluding statement does not reiterate the student's claim.

Source: Common Core State Standards, 2021.

exit tickets, can be quickly analyzed to determine what percentage of the questions the student answered correctly. When students do not meet expectations over the course of several work samples, we can assume that they may need additional support in a skill area.

For larger work samples, such as unit projects and presentations, teachers must utilize clear rubrics that outline the proficiency with which students must achieve the skill. In order to use rubrics as an assessment tool, a teacher would need to identify the specific criteria within the rubric with which the student struggles. A rubric should include two components: the criteria and the expected level of performance on those criteria (Brookhart, 2018). When used as an assessment tool for action research, I recommend using proficiency-based rubrics. This form of rubric uses the same achievement level for both formative and summative assessment and is useful for showing progress on the skill (Brookhart, 2013). Proficiency-based rubrics may be tied to a state academic standard, an IEP goal, or a specific skill or behavior that the student needs to exhibit. Table 2.4 shows an example of a proficiency-based rubric that is tied to a seventh-grade English Language Arts Common Core standard. The specific criteria included in the rubric are the subskills listed in the standard. If using this rubric as an assessment tool for identifying student needs, I recommend considering interventions or additional student supports for criteria in which the student scored at either the "novice" or "learning-in-progress" levels.

OBSERVATIONS

Another form of data, and one that I recommend when students exhibit behavior challenges, is observations of the student. When observing student behavior, teachers must take note of a variety of things, including the behavior itself, what happens before and after the behavior, and any other information that may be important for better understanding the behavior; this information is known as the ABC, or "antecedent-behavior-consequence" (Alberto & Troutman, 2012). In addition, teachers should use specific definitions of the behaviors being observed to ensure that they are tracking the same behaviors each time (Sheaffer et al., 2021). It is critical that behavior observations occur over the course of several days so that you gain a solid understanding of the pattern of behavior during this baseline data collection (Lewis et al., 2014). Observation forms can take a variety of formats, and teachers should choose or design one that meets their specific needs. One option for designing an observation form is the use of a table. In table 2.2, we read about Johnny who "kicks the table and screams." Table 2.5 provides a sample observation form that was used to collect baseline data on this specific behavior.

TABLE 2.5. Sample behavior observation form

Day, time, and location	Behavior	Antecedent	Consequence	Other information
Monday 9:03 a.m. Art classroom	Johnny kicked the art table, knocking over the paints onto the floor. While kicking the table, he screamed, "I hate art!"	The class was paining abstract art in the form of Picasso. Each child was asked to make an abstract face. While Johnny was painting, his paintbrush slipped, causing him to paint a blue line across his paper.	When the paints fell to the floor, they spilled. When Johnny saw the paint on the floor, he began to cry. The teacher helped the other students move to the other side of the room while the paraprofessional sat with Johnny. Once Johnny calmed down, the paraprofessional helped him clean up the mess.	Just before Johnny painted the line on his paper, the teacher complimented Jin (who was sitting next to Johnny) on his painting.
Monday 11:47 a.m. General education classroom	Johnny stood up, kicked his desk, and screamed, "I can't do math!" and walked out of the room.	Students were working independently on their math assignments while the teacher and the classroom paraprofessional walked around the room, assisting students as needed.	Johnny walked down the hall and into the restroom. The teacher followed him and waited for him outside the restroom. When Johnny came out, he saw the teacher and (unprompted) apologized to her for his behavior and then explained that the math assignment was so hard and made him feel frustrated.	Johnny has a diagnosed learning disability in math.
Tuesday 11:41 a.m. General education classroom	Johnny leaned back in his chair and began to kick at his desk.	Students were working independently on their math assignments while the teacher and the classroom paraprofessional walked around the room, assisting students as needed.	The teacher went over to Johnny and asked him to take 10 deep breaths with her. When they were done, taking breaths, Johnny put his head down on his desk until the end of class.	Johnny has a diagnosed learning disability in math.

SURVEYS/QUESTIONNAIRES

Depending on the specific skill or challenge that you are addressing, surveys may be an appropriate form of data collection. Surveys can be an effective tool for gaining information on a specific topic from a large group of people, but surveys must be created with intentionality (Jones et al., 2013). Surveys can also be useful for gathering information from a smaller number of people quickly. For special education action research, surveys may be used for understanding the needs of a large group of stakeholders or can be used to understand information about a few students in a class. For example, a school district special education department may want to get a better understanding of what parents across the district need in order to support their children's learning and progress toward

---

TEXTBOX 2.2
SAMPLE SURVEY FOR FUN FRIDAY IN
THE SPECIAL EDUCATION CLASSROOM

This week, we will be celebrating your hard work this semester by having a Fun Friday celebration! In order to plan for this event, I need your help. Please vote for your favorites by circling one item from each category below.

Movie
Toy Story
Happy Feet
The Incredibles

Game
Apples to Apples
Sorry
Headbanz

Sweet Treat
Mini cupcakes (chocolate and vanilla)
Cookies (chocolate chip and sugar)
Brownies

Salty Treat
Popcorn
Pretzels
Chips

Healthy Treat
Apple slices
Carrot sticks
String cheese

IEP goals at home. A large survey can be an efficient way to gather this data. On a small scale, a special educator may be planning a "Fun Friday" and want to know students' preferences for activities and snacks. A survey can help the teacher quickly gain this information. Textbox 2.2 offers a sample Fun Friday survey.

The specific wording of survey questions may impact participant answers; questions must be clearly worded to avoid jargon words, not include terms that could be considered biased or offensive and only ask one piece of information per question (Pew Research Center, 2021). In addition, survey questions that are very specific will result in more accurate data as all survey respondents are likely to interpret the question similarly (Colorado State University, 2021). You will notice that in the Fun Friday survey, I listed the flavors of cupcakes and cookies so that students knew exactly what was being offered. Survey questions may be close-ended, where participants are asked to select from a list of responses, or they may be open-ended and allow participants to write their own response to the question (Pew Research Center, 2021). Closed-ended questions can be analyzed more quickly but may not offer the specific information that a teacher researcher is seeking. Keep in mind that you may choose to include both close-ended and open-ended questions in the survey (Colorado State University, 2021).

In addition to surveys for gaining information, as mentioned at the beginning of this section, teacher may also consider using pre-test/post-test surveys to better understand stakeholder perceptions of an intervention. The pre-test/post-test method may be used to evaluate how a specific lesson or learning unit impacted student understanding or perceptions of a specific concept (Delucchi, 2014). The pre-test offers the baseline data, which is then compared to the post-test to evaluate the impact of the intervention (Sanders, 2019; Simkins & Allen, 2000). It is critical that the pre-test and post-test are identical in terms of formatting and delivery; for example, if the pre-test is given in paper/pencil format, the post-test should also be completed on paper (Sanders, 2019). Textbox 2.3 provides a sample survey for evaluating student learning on the topic of states

---

TEXTBOX 2.3
SAMPLE SURVEY FOR EVALUATING STUDENT LEARNING

States and Capitals Learning Check

Write the capital for each of the states below.

Alabama _____ . New York _____ .

Colorado _____ . Pennsylvania _____ .

Florida _____ . Texas _____ .

Kansas _____ . Wisconsin _____ .

---

and capitals. You will notice that this example is very basic; keep in mind that even basic assessments can effectively evaluate student learning. It is not necessary for teachers to spend a lot of time developing assessments.

CHECKLISTS

For some academic skills, teachers may consider using a checklist to collect data (see figure 1.1). A checklist is simply a list of specific skills; the teacher puts a checkmark next to the ones the student has mastered (Reeves, 2011). Checklists can be useful for collecting data on concepts that include many distinct skills. One example of a skill that would be appropriate for evaluating through the use of a checklist is mathematics addition facts. When teaching young learners, teachers need to know what mathematics facts the students know and need a simple tool for keeping track of initial knowledge, as well as ongoing progress.

In addition to being used for academic skills, checklists are also useful for evaluating and tracking behavior concerns. Behavior checklists can be used to

Math Fact	Correct	Incorrect
0 + 1		
1 + 1		
2 + 1		
3 + 1		
4 + 1		
5 + 1		
6 +1		
7 + 1		
8 + 1		
9 + 1		

FIGURE 2.1. Sample Checklist for Evaluating Student Knowledge of +1 Mathematics Addition Facts

Task	Yes	No
Student turns on hot water.		
Student turns on cold water.		
Student puts their hands under water for at least 5 seconds.		
Student puts one pump of soap into their hands.		
Student rubs hands together to ensure that palms are covered with soap.		
Student rubs soap on the top of their left hand.		
Student rubs soap on the top of their right hand.		
Student places both hands under the water.		

FIGURE 2.2. Sample Checklist for Evaluating Student Handwashing Skills

identify a particular aspect of one challenging behavior or to identify all problematic behaviors that a student exhibits. Commonly used behavior checklists include *The Child Behavior Checklist* (CBCL) and the *Behavior Problem Checklist* (BPC), but teachers can also choose to make their own checklists.

Special education teachers may also use checklists to evaluate students' ability to complete a functional life skill. Figure 2.2 offers a checklist that a special educator might use to evaluate a student's handwashing skills. In order to create this checklist, the teacher must first create a task analysis of the steps of handwashing and include each step in the checklist. A task analysis involves breaking down a task into individual steps and listing each step required to complete the task (Szidon & Franzone, 2009).

When using a checklist for data collection purposes, I recommend having multiple stakeholders complete the same checklist for the student. Getting responses from various people and sources will provide you with a more thorough picture of the academic or behavior challenge.

RATING SCALES

Another data collection option, similar to a checklist, is a rating scale. When using a rating scale, a special education teacher evaluates a student's abilities on discrete skills using a scale that indicates the extent to which the student can successfully complete the skill (Campbell & Hammond, 2014). Rating scales can also be used to evaluate the severity of a behavior that a student is exhibiting (Cox, 2019). A rating scale is like a checklist in that it identifies whether or not a student can complete a skill, but it provides additional information regarding the behavior or skill (Whitcomb, 2018). Using rate scales can be beneficial when teachers want to know if a student is making progress toward mastering a skill or whether a behavior challenge is becoming less severe. Rating scales

TABLE 2.6. Sample rating scale for evaluating student learning behaviors

Please rate the extent to which the student exhibited the following behaviors in each category during each subject.

1 = Never; 3 = Sometimes; 5 = Always or almost always

Subject	Facing forward and looking in Direction of Teacher	Feet on floor	Hands to self	Actively participating in class (raising hand, completing work. etc.)
Mathematics	1 2 3 4 5	1 2 3 4 5	1 2 3 4 5	1 2 3 4 5
Reading	1 2 3 4 5	1 2 3 4 5	1 2 3 4 5	1 2 3 4 5
Spelling	1 2 3 4 5	1 2 3 4 5	1 2 3 4 5	1 2 3 4 5
Writing	1 2 3 4 5	1 2 3 4 5	1 2 3 4 5	1 2 3 4 5
Social studies	1 2 3 4 5	1 2 3 4 5	1 2 3 4 5	1 2 3 4 5
Science	1 2 3 4 5	1 2 3 4 5	1 2 3 4 5	1 2 3 4 5
Specials	1 2 3 4 5	1 2 3 4 5	1 2 3 4 5	1 2 3 4 5

should include an odd number of options so that a midpoint choice is available (Weijters et al., 2010). Table 2.6 shows a rating scale that a teacher might use to evaluate appropriate student learning behaviors in the classroom.

INTERVIEWS

Another form of data collection that can be especially beneficial for behavior and attention is the use of interviews. Interviews can also be a good way to collect data on the perceptions, experiences, or ideas of students, teachers, paraprofessionals, parents, or other school stakeholders through individualized verbal responses (Abualsaud, 2019). Interviews may be structured, semistructured or unstructured, depending on the specific information the teacher researcher is aiming to learn. In a structured interview, the teacher will ask predetermined questions and the exact same questions will be asked to each person interviewed in the same order and the same manner (Gill et al., 2008). In a semistructured interview, the teacher will begin with a list of questions, but may select to only ask some questions from the list, add additional questions based on the interviewee's answers, ask the questions in a different order for each interviewee, or make other changes to the interview protocol during the interview (Abualsaud, 2019). An unstructured interview occurs when the teacher has an idea regarding the general topic that they want to discuss, but the questions are created during the interview itself based on the answers to previous questions (Gill et al., 2008).

Because conducting interviews can be very time consuming, a teacher will generally only interview a small number of people when using this data collection tool. Interviews are often used in combination with other data collection sources in the classroom (Natow, 2019). It is important that the teacher

---

TEXTBOX 2.4
SAMPLE SEMI-STRUCTURED STUDENT INTERVIEW

What are your favorite things about school?

What are your biggest challenges in school?

How do you think having a learning disability affects you in schools?

What support do you need to be successful in school?

What do you do to help yourself succeed?

What can teachers do to help you?

When you leave school, what do you like to do?

Tell me about your family.

Tell me about any sports teams or clubs you participate in.

---

researcher takes good notes or records the interview for later transcription in order to ensure that they accurately capture the information provided by the interviewee (Jamshed, 2014). For special educators, interviews can be used to gain a variety of information from stakeholders. One way that a teacher might use an interview is to gain information from a student in preparation for an IEP meeting. It is critical that student input is included in the IEP, but student attendance and participation at the IEP meeting is not always feasible, especially for younger learners or for students who may be intimidated by talking during the meetings. Textbox 2.4 offers a sample semistructured interview that a teacher might use to gain student input in advance of an annual review IEP meeting.

THE CHALLENGE WITH ONLY RELYING ON FORMAL ASSESSMENTS

For many academic skills, teachers have access to both formal and informal data. While the formal data, from standardized tests and other large-scale assessment tools, can provide good information and help us to identify students who may need additional support in a specific subject area, the formal data should not be the only data collected. Teachers should pair formal data with informal data when determining students' baseline levels and progress during an intervention. Consider the scenario of Rafael, mentioned in table 2.2. The Development Reading Assessment (DRA) is a commonly used standardized tool for assessing the reading fluency, story retell, and reading comprehension of students in kindergarten through eighth grade (Toyama et al., 2017). Rafael reads at a level of 10 on the DRA2, which indicates that he is reading at the level we would expect a first grader to read midyear (Beaver & Carter, 2006). While we may look at Rafael's score and assume that he is reading below grade level, we may be wrong if we don't look at other data to verify our assumption. Some children experience significant levels of anxiety when taking standardized tests (Segool et al., 2013); this anxiety can impact their test scores and inaccurately indicate low academic achievement (Liew et al., 2014).

DATA LITERACY

"Data literacy" is a term used to describe the act of making classroom decisions based on data (Mandinach & Gummer, 2013). In order to do this, teachers must be experts in data-driven decision making, which involves summarizing and synthesizing information from various research-based sources and using that information to guide instructional practices (Green et al., 2016). We sometimes talk about triangulating data. When we triangulate data, we simply take three unique pieces of information and look for connections and trends (Venables,

2013). For example, a teacher might conduct an observation, look at student work samples, and interview the student's parents to better understand a student's learning needs.

ADDITIONAL DATA COLLECTION CONSIDERATIONS

As you prepare to take data, you should remember that many factors can impact a student's academic performance or behavior on any given day. Not enough sleep the night before, wearing an itchy sweater, a buzzing sound coming from the classroom lights, being hungry, or any number of other experiences can have an impact on how a student performs.

It is critical that you have a plan for ensuring immediate recording of data as the research indicates that classroom data collection is more accurate when teachers record the data immediately following the student's behavior challenge instead of waiting until the end of the class period or school day to do so (Jasper & Taber-Doughty, 2015; Taber-Doughty & Jasper, 2012).

FORMING A PROBLEM STATEMENT

Once you have collected your baseline data, you will use that data to develop a problem statement. The problem statement describes the "why" of your research (Newman & Covrig, 2013). Specifically, it serves a few purposes. First, it provides an explanation of the context in which the problem exists (McGahie et al., 2001) and a framework for the work you are doing (Al-Riyami, 2008). Third, it explains why the research project is worthy of the time it will require to complete (Maxwell & Loomis, 2003). I recommend, though, that teachers acknowledge in the problem statement that the intervention may or may not be effective by using terms such as "may" instead of "will." Finally, the problem statement explains the problem itself in specific terms. In addition to identifying the problem, you must also provide a rationale for why the problem matters. Textbox 2.5 provides examples of sample problem statements that would be appropriate for special education teacher action research; in addition, the case studies in appendix A offer problem statements.

CONCLUSION

Data collection is an essential component of being a special education teacher action researcher. Data-based decision making is critical for ensuring that you can meet the unique needs of all students. In this chapter, you learned a variety of strategies for collecting data. Good data collection strategies include

TEXTBOX 2.5
SAMPLE PROBLEM STATEMENTS WITH RATIONALE

Johnny throws a tantrum, which includes yelling and kicking the chair, when he is asked to sit at the table to do table work. These tantrums are disruptive to the learning of the other children in the classroom, and they keep Johnny from learning. I want to conduct this action research because I believe that it may help Johnny be more successful and support the learning of the other children.

Penelope is an eleventh grader who is identified with an intellectual disability and receives instruction in a self-contained classroom. She struggles to understand money and financial decision making. Penelope has expressed that she wants to live independently and have a job in the community after she leaves school. In order to do this, she will need to understand the value of both bills and coins, how to use money to pay for items, and how to budget her money in order to ensure her needs are met. This action research may help Penelope gain the skills to manage money effectively.

Rafael is a third-grade student and reads at DRA level of 10. This means that he is reading about two years below grade-level expectation and is unable to read the third-grade content in all subject areas. Reading on grade level (or closer to grade level) may support Rafael in achieving the state academic standards, especially in the areas of language arts, science, and social studies.

Asa is a seventh-grade student who is frequently tardy to her classes. So far this school year, she has been tardy to 65% of her classes. Asa is most frequently tardy to her morning classes and the first class after lunch. Being tardy to class means that Asa misses instruction and disrupts the learning of the other students when she arrives late. I want to conduct this action research because I believe that it may help Asa arrive to her classes on time.

assessments, work samples, observations, interviews, surveys, checklists, and rating scales. Through collecting baseline data and triangulating that data, you can begin to better support your learners.

REVIEW QUESTIONS AND EXERCISES

1. As a teacher, what difference does it make that you have data to support your decisions? In the classroom, what is the difference between an opinion and a belief based on data? How will you ensure that you are making decisions based on data-based information and not just your own opinion (or the opinions of those around you)?

2. Using table 2.2 as an example, write five examples and nonexamples of learning or behavior challenges that a student with a disability might exhibit in the classroom.

3. Table 2.5 is a sample observation form. Using that form, create one of your own and conduct a 15-minute observation. You may observe a student in a classroom, a family member, or a stranger in a public place.

4. After completing the observation, write a short paragraph about your experience with a specific focus on the challenges of observation. In addition, be sure that you consider what you learned about conducting an observation and how that learning will impact you as a teacher.

5. Figure 2.2 is a task analysis checklist for handwashing. Choose a discrete skill that you might teach in your classroom. Create a task analysis checklist for that skill, using figure 2.2 as a guide.

6. Thinking about the data collection tools presented in this chapter, consider the pros and cons of each one. Create a visual representation to show this information.

7. Textbox 2.5 provides sample problem statements for academic and behavior challenges you might encounter in your classroom. Using the textbox as a guide, write five additional problem statements that might be appropriate for a student in a special education classroom.

Identifying Potential Evidence-Based Interventions

. . . .

Student Learning Objectives

After reading chapter 3 and completing the exercises at the end of the chapter, students will be able to:

- Identify the impacts of action research on student learning and behavior outcomes
- Describe the purpose of evidence-based practices within the action research process
- Identify evidence-based practices that may support the needs of students in their own classrooms
- Design an intervention plan for supporting a student's learning or behavior needs

Mr. Bullock has begun work on his action research project and has been taking data on Billy's kicking behaviors. Mr. Bullock knows that it is important to consider multiple sources of data in order to get a more thorough picture of Billy's needs, so he has observed Billy over several days and interviewed Billy, his brother, and their parents. By looking at all this data, Mr. Bullock hypothesizes that Billy kicks his brother when he is frustrated because he does not know a more acceptable way to manage his frustrations. Mr. Bullock created the following problem statement: "Billy kicks his brother, causing pain and injury to him. This behavior seems to occur when Billy is frustrated that he is unable to complete a task or when things do not go his way. I want to conduct this action research to support Billy in finding an appropriate way to manage his frustrations and to keep his brother safe." Now that he has developed a problem statement, Mr. Bullock is ready to move on to the next step of his action research project.

. . . .

In chapter 2, we talked about using data to better understand a student's learning or behavior needs and then using that data to develop a problem statement that identifies the specific need, as well as an explanation of why the challenge must be addressed. Like Mr. Bullock, you have likely completed this step of your action research. You have identified a student learning or behavior challenge, collected baseline data, and developed a problem statement that clearly identifies the challenge and why it is problematic. Now that you have done this, it is time to find an intervention that might be appropriate for the specific needs of your student. Doing this will require you to identify evidence-based interventions.

EVIDENCE-BASED PRACTICES

If you have spent some time in a school in the past few years, I suspect you have heard the phrase "evidence-based practices," or the acronym EBPs. The term "evidence-based practices" is frequently used in education settings, but it is not well understood. So, what is an evidence-based practice and why should you as a teacher use them? An evidence-based practice is an instructional strategy or intervention that has proven to be effective for student learning over multiple research studies (Bittner & Davis, 2019). This means that several researchers have studied the effectiveness of the strategy and the data they have collected proves (or highly suggests) that the practice works as intended. The key to knowing whether a strategy is an evidence-based practice is finding out whether there is repeated research on its use. The teacher in the classroom next door saying that the practice works does not make it an EBP. Your favorite educator writing a blog post or tweeting about the practice does not make it an EBP. Seeing dozens of ideas for implementing a practice when you check Pinterest or Teachers Pay Teachers does not make it an EBP. Only repeated research with reliable and reproducible data can lead to a teaching practice being classified as an EBP.

Now that you know what the term "evidence-based practice" means, let's talk about why you need to use them. The first reason that you need to use EBPs is that their use is mandated by law. Both the Individuals with Disabilities Education Act of 2004 (IDEA, 2004) and the Every Student Succeeds Act (ESSA, 2015) mandate that schools use evidence-based practices to support student learning and improve academic and behavioral outcomes. For students with disabilities, IDEA mandates that special educators use strategies supported by peer-reviewed research (Bittner & Davis, 2019). Peer review occurs when a research study and its findings are reviewed and scrutinized by other experts in the field to determine if the research was conducted ethically and using best research practices, as well as whether the results are reported appropriately (Kelly et al., 2014). If the peer reviewers conclude that the research was not well conducted or inaccurately reported, it will not be published (Beall, 2017). This process helps to ensure that good practices are identified and articles about ineffective instructional practices are not published in research journals.

The second reason teachers must use EBPs is that we know they work. For all students, but especially students with disabilities, it is critical that we do not waste any learning time by using ineffective instruction. Our students deserve the best instruction we can give them. By using EBPs in the classroom, we can feel confident that we are providing the high-quality instruction our students need to be successful.

As I am writing this chapter, there is a discussion happening on Twitter (my favorite place to discuss education-related topics) regarding evidence-based practices. The initial tweet said that an evidence-based practice should be viewed as a verb, not a noun. The point of the conversation is that an EBP is more than just a strategy. EBPs are effective when they involve intentional and systematic action by teachers. Evidence-based practices work because dedicated teachers select the practices that are most appropriate for their students, implement them as intended, and take data to ensure that the practice is working for students. As you conduct your action research, think about this idea—your actions are a critical part of the success of an academic or behavioral intervention.

LOCATING EBPS

Now that you know what the term "evidence-based practice" means, you need to know how to locate EBPs to support the success of your students. When researching appropriate EBPs, you will need to think about the problem statement you wrote at the end of chapter 2. That problem statement included a description of the student learning or behavior challenge. When looking for an EBP, you will need to identify practices that have proven to be effective for addressing the specific challenge of your student. Textbox 2.5 in chapter 2 offered a list of sample problem statements that a special educator might write. Table 3.1 offers a list of EBPs that may be appropriate for supporting the mock students from these problem statements.

Now that you have seen examples of EBPs for a few common classroom challenges, you may be wondering how you will find potential strategies to implement with your students. If you are currently a university student, you likely have access to peer-reviewed research journals through your university library; a search of the library database is a great place to start. Common journal databases to which your university might have access include EBSCO, JSTOR, and Academic Search. Each of these databases have access to thousands of journal articles and you can locate research that is relevant to your action research through conducting a simple database search. To do this, you will want to

TABLE 3.1. Evidence-based practices for learners

Student learning or behavior challenge	Sample evidence-based practices
Johnny throws a tantrum when asked to sit at the table to do work.	Rewards for sitting at the table and working (Foley et al., 2019) Prompting to sit at the table and complete the work (DiCarlo et al., 2017) Choice of where to complete work (Howell et al., 2019)
Penelope struggles to understand money.	Community-based instruction (Barczak, 2019) Modified schema-based instruction (Root et al., 2017) Concrete-representational-abstract approach (Bouck, et al., 2017)
Rafael reads below grade level.	Systematic phonics instruction (Ehri, 2020) Technology-based small group tutoring (Madden & Slavin, 2017) Listening to passage read aloud paired with repeated readings (Lee & Yoon, 2017)
Asa is frequently tardy to class.	Offering rewards/incentives for on-time attendance to class (Freeman et al., 2018) Self-monitoring of arrival time (Bruhn et al., 2015) Group contingency/classwide reward for Asa's on-time arrival to class (Hulac & Benson, 2010)

identify keywords for your search and be sure to indicate in the search options that you only want "peer-reviewed" articles. In addition, I suggest limiting the publication dates to the past five or ten years to ensure that you are looking at the most recent research on the topic. Table 3.2 offers suggested search terms that could be used for the student scenarios presented in textbox 2.5 and table 3.1.

As you search for articles, you may find that your search terms yield few results. In these cases, you will want to expand your search. You can do this in a few ways. First, you can increase the publication dates to look for research that is older than the five or ten years I suggested. However, if you do this, you will still want to have some recent research to examine for your action research. The other way to expand your search is to think more broadly with your search terms. Consider terms related to the specific student need. For example, look at the search term options for Asa in table 3.2. The specific action research focus to support Asa is addressing her tardiness to class. However, a database search with the term "tardiness in high school" yielded no results, so the action researcher had to think more broadly. Tardiness is a behavior concern, so the researcher chose to use "behavior interventions" as a search term. Additionally, the researcher knows that tardiness and school attendance are often related, so she chose to also look at research regarding school attendance. By expanding

TABLE 3.2.   Search terms for locating research in an academic database

Student	Potential search terms
Johnny	"Physical aggression in the classroom" "Task avoidant behaviors"
Penelope	"Academic intervention" "Intellectual disability" "Teaching financial literacy to students with disabilities"
Rafael	"Reading interventions" "Reading instruction"
Asa	"Behavior interventions in high school" "School attendance"

the search terms, the action researcher was able to find relevant research for the project.

FINDING EBPS WITHOUT ACCESS TO A UNIVERSITY DATABASE

If you are not currently a university student or your library has limited access to journals, it can be more challenging to locate evidence-based practices. But it is not impossible! One way to gain access to peer-reviewed articles is by being a member of a special education professional organization, such as the Council for Exceptional Children, TASH, the Council for Learning Disabilities, or the American Council on Rural Special Education. Each of these organizations publishes peer-reviewed research journals and membership includes access to either print or electronic versions of these journals. In addition, some of these organizations also have a specific journal that is written for teachers and other practitioners. These journals include research-to-practice articles that explain research on specific EBPs in easy-to-understand terms and offer specific recommendations for classroom implementation. Even though these journals do not publish research studies, they are still peer-reviewed and the articles provide an overview of existing research on the specific topic. Articles published in these journals are trustworthy and can help teachers quickly identify potential interventions for supporting student learning. Table 3.3 is a list of some practitioner journals that are published by special education professional organizations. In addition to these journals, I recommend that special educators consider becoming members of the National Association of Special Education Teachers, which offers hundreds of practical articles about EBPs in the member section of their website.

If you are not a member of a professional organization or are unable to find the information you are seeking through the journals you receive, there

TABLE 3.3. Practitioner journals published by SPED professional organizations

Journal name	About the journal	Website
Teaching Exceptional Children	This is the practitioner journal for the Council for Exceptional Children (CEC), and all CEC members receive a copy six times per year. Articles cover a variety of topics related to meeting the needs of students with disabilities.	https://journals.sagepub.com/home/tcx
Inclusive Practices	This is the practitioner journal for TASH and is published four times per year. Articles focus on supporting the needs of persons with significant disabilities across the lifespan.	https://us.sagepub.com/en-us/nam/inclusive-practices/journal203704
Young Exceptional Children	This is the practitioner journal for the CEC Division for Early Childhood (DEC) and is published quarterly. Articles focus on supporting children with disabilities from birth through age 8.	https://journals.sagepub.com/home/yec
Beyond Behavior	This is the practitioner journal for the CEC Division of Emotional and Behavioral Health (DEBH) and is published three times per year. Articles focus on teaching students with emotional disturbances and behavior challenges.	https://journals.sagepub.com/home/bbx
Intervention in School and Clinic	This journal is published by the Council for Learning Disabilities (CLD) and issues are released five times per year. Articles focus on meeting the needs of students with learning disabilities, as well as students with emotional disturbances.	https://journals.sagepub.com/home/isc

are free online options for accessing some special education EBPs. The first place that I suggest you look is the IRIS Center (https://iris.peabody.vanderbilt.edu/), housed at Vanderbilt University. This federally funded organization offers learning modules and other resources that help special educators understand evidence-based practices for supporting students with disabilities. Plus, their social media game is on-point; I recommend following the IRIS Center on

Facebook or Twitter to stay up to date on their newest offerings and to get some good laughs!

If the IRIS Center does not offer you the information you need or you want additional information, your next stop should be the ERIC database (https://eric.ed.gov/). ERIC is funded through the U.S. Department of Education and provides full text articles, presentations, and other materials. When you use this database, you will need to use search terms related to your topic as discussed earlier in the chapter. In addition, you will need to click the box on the search screen that says "peer-reviewed only."

Other websites that offer information on special education evidence-based practices are listed in table 3.4. However, when choosing to use these websites, keep in mind that it is still best practice for you as a teacher researcher to locate the actual research studies and read them. Relying on these secondary sources should be a starting point to help guide you as you look for peer reviewed research.

In addition to the websites and other tools listed above, you can also access peer-reviewed research and practitioner articles via open-access education journals. Open access means that they are available online and are free to access. You will want to be careful, though, if you are looking for EBPs via open-access journals as there are an increasing number of predatory journals that claim to publish peer-reviewed research, but in reality, will publish any article as long as the authors will pay to have it published (Beall, 2010). In the field of special education, reputable open-access journals generally do not charge authors to publish their work, so one way to identify a predatory journal is to look at the website for the cost of publication. In table 3.5, I offer recommendations for

TABLE 3.4. Websites for locating special education EBPs

Name	Weblink
High Leverage Practices for Students With Disabilities	https://highleveragepractices.org/
CEEDAR Center	https://ceedar.education.ufl.edu/
Autism Focused Intervention Resources and Modules	https://afirm.fpg.unc.edu/node/137
Center on Positive Behavioral Interventions and Supports	https://www.pbis.org/
Collaborative for Academic, Social, and Emotional Learning (CASEL)	https://casel.org/
National Technical Assistance Center on Transition	https://transitionta.org/
OSEP Ideas That Work	https://osepideasthatwork.org/
What Works Clearinghouse	https://ies.ed.gov/ncee/wwc

TABLE 3.5.   Peer-Reviewed Open Access SPED Journals & Newsletters

Journal name	About the journal	Website
Journal of Special Education Apprenticeship	This peer-reviewed journal offers both research and practitioner articles that focus on supporting persons with disabilities across the lifespan. Article authors are generally Special education doctoral students or early career professors.	http://www.josea.info/web/public/
Special Education: Research, Policy, & Practice	This peer-reviewed journal is published once per year by Hofstra University. All articles are research related to persons with disabilities.	https://www.hofstra.edu/academics/colleges/soeahs/sped/sped_special-education-research-policy-practice.html
International Journal of Early Childhood Special Education	This international peer-reviewed journal is published twice annually. Articles focus on children with disabilities from birth through age eight.	https://www.int-jecse.net/index.php
Sage Open	This peer-reviewed journal publishes research articles on a variety of topics related to education.	https://journals.sagepub.com/home/sgo
LD Forum	This peer-reviewed bimonthly newsletter is published by the Council for Learning Disabilities. Most issues include a peer-reviewed article on a topic related to supporting students with learning disabilities or an emotional disturbance.	https://council-for-learning-disabilities.org/learning-disability-forum-council-learning-disabilities-newletter/
T-CARE	This peer-reviewed newsletter is published once or twice per year. Articles are short and written for teachers, with practical tips for implementing research and best practices in special education instruction.	https://www.csun.edu/center-teaching-learning/publications

some open-access, peer-reviewed journals that special educators may use to locate evidence-based practices for their action research.

In addition to the options listed in this section for locating peer-reviewed research, you can also use Google Scholar to identify potential research articles that you want to read. Generally, Google Scholar does not provide access to the full text of an article. Instead, you can see just the abstract. However, if you find an article on Google Scholar that you would like to read and you cannot access in another manner, you can email the article author and ask for a copy. Most special education researchers are more than happy to share their research with teachers. Keep in mind, though, that it may take several days (or more) to receive a response from the article author, so be patient and plan for this process to take time.

A final option that you may choose is to read books on the topic. However, I recommend that you do this with caution, knowing that books are generally not peer-reviewed and many are self-published, which means that a person can write a book of ideas for teachers that are not supported by research and may, in fact, be harmful to children. In addition, even books that include EBPs are secondary sources. The books are meant to help bridge the "research to practice gap" and get the information into the hands of stakeholders. But, as a researcher, your job is to be looking at the actual research, so books should not be your primary source for locating EBPs.

As you research evidence-based practices in these various locations, you will find that there are often several practices that might be appropriate for your student. I recommend creating a list of potential EBPs that might be options. If you look at table 3.1, you will notice that I listed multiple potential interventions for each student. You will want to do the same thing. In the next section of this chapter, we will discuss how to determine if the intervention(s) you located may be appropriate for your student.

DETERMINING THE APPROPRIATENESS OF AN EBP FOR YOUR STUDENT

After you have researched EBPs that might support your student, you will need to consider which strategy to try first for your action research. You will do this by considering the appropriateness of each strategy for the specific needs of your student and your classroom. When it comes to effective interventions for students with disabilities, there is no one-size-fits all approach. An intervention that works for one student may not be appropriate for another student, even to address the same learning or behavior need.

When determining the appropriateness of the intervention, the first thing to consider is the populations on which the intervention has been researched. If the participants in the studies are similar to your student, the intervention may be appropriate. If the study participants are very different from your student, I recommend implementing the intervention with caution. For example, your student may be a first grader with autism who is refusing to sit on the carpet at circle time and the intervention research you have located focuses on kindergarten students with autism who refuse to sit at the table. In this case, your student and his need are similar to the students and need in the research study, so there is a high likelihood that the intervention you are considering will be appropriate for your student. Conversely, if you are looking for an intervention for that same first grader and considering a strategy based on research you have found that included only a tenth grader with an emotional disturbance who refuses to sit with the class, you would want to look for more research literature before deciding to try the intervention for your student. The tenth grader is a different age and has a different disability than your student.

A second consideration is the resources that will be needed to implement the intervention. Think about whether the intervention requires technology tools or other materials. Do you have access to these materials? If not, can you get access? In addition, think about the personnel resources that are required to implement the intervention. There are many evidence-based practices for students with disabilities that require one-to-one instruction for several hours per day. While these interventions may be appropriate for your student, they may not be practical. Unless the student has a one-to-one paraprofessional written into their IEP, it is unlikely that you will be able to try one of these interventions. If you do not have access to the resources necessary for implementing an intervention as outlined in the research, I recommend finding another EBP to try.

A third thing to consider is whether the intervention has already been attempted to support this child for this specific need. If the intervention has been tried before, look at the data and talk to other stakeholders to find out why it was not successful and/or why it was discontinued. Was it implemented as intended? Did it have a small impact but not enough of an impact? Did it cause a problem with other students in the classroom? Were the adults in charge of implementation uncomfortable with the intervention? As you think about each of these questions, consider whether the answers lead you to try the intervention again or whether there is sufficient evidence to indicate that the intervention may not work for this child.

Next, consider whether the intervention is ethical and respectful of the student and all other stakeholders. There is a chance that you will find research to support interventions that might get results but should not be implemented. For example, some schools used to spray water into the faces of children with autism to stop self-injurious behaviors (Bailey et al., 1983). While this intervention may have been effective at stopping the behaviors, it was not respectful of the students and is no longer considered an appropriate intervention. When you look at interventions you found in the research, consider whether they are ethical and respectful.

Finally, consider whether you are willing to implement the intervention as intended. There are some interventions that are effective, require few resources, and are respectful, but can still be challenging to implement. One example is the use of planned ignoring to address attention-seeking behaviors. When we ignore these behaviors, they will get worse before they get better (Hester et al., 2009). And, sometimes, the behaviors will get very extreme before the intervention of planned ignoring becomes effective. It can be hard for teachers to ignore these extreme behaviors, so when a teacher wants to use this intervention, I recommend taking time to consider whether they are prepared to do what is required. When considering an intervention, be sure to understand what could happen and make sure that you are willing to implement with fidelity before you commit to using the EBP for your action research.

Textbox 3.1 includes these questions in a simple list that you can use to determine the appropriateness of an EBP you located in the research. I suggest answering each of these questions for each EBP that you have located to determine which one might be the most appropriate.

DESIGNING AN INTERVENTION PLAN

After you have selected which intervention may be most appropriate, you will need to create a plan for implementing the intervention. Solid planning is needed for success in student learning, so don't skip this step. Take the time you need to develop a solid and realistic plan for implementing the intervention you have selected. This planning process is a great time to solicit support from colleagues and other IEP team members regarding logistics.

Because this action research is only one of many responsibilities you have in your classroom, I recommend keeping your plan as simple as possible, while still implementing the intervention with fidelity. Fidelity is just a fancy word for saying that you implement the intervention as designed in the research literature and do not adapt it unnecessarily. For example, if you have selected

TABLE 3.6. Sample Intervention Plan

Step	Who is responsible?	Other information
Create homework passes.	Teacher	The teacher will design the homework pass and print twenty copies.
Discuss with Asa the intervention plan so that she understands that she will get a reward for arriving to class on time.	Teacher	This must be done the day before the intervention begins.
Give Asa a homework pass as she walks into the classroom, on days that she arrives on time.	Teacher initially, but eventually Asa	Plan to slowly fade out teacher involvement in this step. Homework passes will be kept in a folder by the classroom door. After a few weeks, Asa will become responsible for picking up a homework pass as she enters the classroom. If she forgets to pick it up, she does not receive the pass that day.
Take data on the number of days each week that Asa arrives on time.	Teacher initially, but eventually Asa	Plan to slowly fade out teacher involvement in this step. After the second week of the intervention, Asa will be required to email the teacher every Friday to report how many days she arrived to the class on time that week. If she neglects to send the email, she loses one homework pass.
Submit the homework pass in lieu of submitting class assignments.	Asa	Asa can choose which assignments she wants to replace with the homework passes she earns
Accept the homework pass in lieu of assignments.	Teacher	Teacher reserves the right to determine that certain assignments cannot be replaced with a homework pass
Ensure that there are always homework passes in the folder.	Teacher/Asa	Asa is responsible for telling teacher when there are only a few passes left. Teacher is responsible for printing more and putting them in the folder.
Evaluating effectiveness of intervention.	Teacher/Asa	Teacher will compare baseline and intervention data (number of days that Asa arrived on time for class vs. number of days that she did not). Asa will be asked to share her thoughts on the intervention.

to provide Asa (from table 3.1) with a free homework pass each time that she arrives to class on time, you must give her this pass every single time. If you only give her the homework pass when you remember or when you feel like doing it, the intervention may not work, and you are not implementing the reward intervention with fidelity.

As you design your plan, make sure to include the specific action steps that will be taken and who is responsible for each component of the plan. Keep in mind that you, as the teacher, do not have to take responsibility for every aspect of the intervention plan—paraprofessionals, other school personnel, families, and students can all also have responsibilities as appropriate. Additionally, you should include information about data collection and your plan for assessing the effectiveness of the intervention. Remember to keep your plan as simple

TABLE 3.7. Common barriers to intervention implementation fidelity

Barrier	Potential solutions
Lack of time	• Ask for help from other stakeholders in implementing the intervention • Ask other school personnel to help with other responsibilities so that teacher has more time for intervention • Select different intervention that might be less time consuming
Lack of resources	• Request needed resources from school district • Request needed resources from school PTA • Request needed resources from outside agencies or grants • Consider making own materials, if possible
Paraprofessionals not following intervention plan	• Provide explicit training to paraprofessionals on how to implement intervention, as well as the research supporting its use • Explain to paraprofessional that implementation fidelity is part of their job • Request assistance from school administration
Jealousy from other students (especially common when an intervention involves rewards)	• Remind students that everyone gets their needs met and that everyone's needs are not the same; "fair is not equal, and equal is not fair" • Design rewards for the whole class • Consider rewarding the entire class for intervention success
Teacher being absent from the classroom	Designate another school personnel (such as a paraprofessional or other teacher) to implement intervention Have students responsible for intervention implementation to the extent possible

and as easy to understand as possible. Table 3.6 offers an example of an intervention plan that Asa's teacher might use to support Asa in consistently arriving to class on time.

As noted earlier, the reality is that one action research intervention in your classroom is only a small portion of your daily responsibilities. And, like other aspects of teaching, you will face barriers and challenges in implementing the intervention, so you should plan for those. As you make plans for the intervention implementation, consider any barriers that might arise and prevent you from implementing the intervention with fidelity; make plans for addressing those barriers. Table 3.7 lists common barriers that arise when implementing interventions, as well as potential solutions for addressing those barriers (but keep in mind that the barriers and solutions in your classroom may be different).

CONCLUSION

It is both best practice and legally mandated to support the learning of students with disabilities through the use of evidence-based interventions. In this chapter, you learned how to identify appropriate interventions for students in your classroom. Interventions should be supported by research and be practical for implementation in your busy classroom. In addition, it is vital that you have a plan for implementing the interventions with fidelity, even in the midst of challenges. Before moving to the next chapter, take some time to investigate EBPs that will support the focus of your action research project. Select an appropriate EBP and design an intervention plan.

REVIEW QUESTIONS AND EXERCISES

1. How does using action research in your classroom ensure that we are not teaching today's students the same as we taught yesterday's students? How does action research ensure that teachers are constantly refining their own instructional practices to support student learning? Why is it important that we are always evaluating our practice and making changes based on the needs of current students? What happens when teachers do not do this?

2. What do you think of the statement that an EBP is a verb, not a noun? What does this mean in practical terms? How does viewing EBPs in this way impact the way in which you approach your action research?

3. Using table 3.1 as an example, select one learning or behavior challenge in your classroom and identify at least three potential EBPs for addressing that challenge. Be sure that the EBPs are supported by peer-reviewed research.

4. Table 3.6 provides a sample intervention plan. Select a student from your classroom (or a mock student), a learning or behavior challenge, and an EBP for addressing that challenge. Create an intervention plan that might support the student. Remember that your plan should be realistic in terms of the time and resources and that you should make plans for addressing potential barriers that may arise.

Implementing an Evidence-Based Intervention

Student Learning Objectives

After reading chapter 4 and completing the exercises at the end of the chapter, students will be able to:

- Identify the considerations that may impact intervention success
- Design a step-by-step intervention plan that uses one or more evidence-based practices (EBPs) to support the learning or behavior needs of a student
- Understand the role of the Institutional Review Board (IRB) and complete a university IRB research study application
- Define the term "implementation fidelity" and explain the importance of this concept when supporting student learning

After collecting the data on Billy's behavior, Mr. Bullock reviewed the data with the help of trusted colleagues. In addition, he asked Billy to share his thoughts on this behavior. After taking all of this information into account, Mr. Bullock believes that an appropriate intervention to implement is proximity control, with the responsibility for implementing the intervention being shared by both Mr. Bullock and one of his paraprofessionals. Proximity control is an evidence-based intervention in which a teacher or other adult keeps a minimal physical distance between themselves and a student, with the intention of helping the student to control challenging behaviors. In addition, Billy will receive a reward of his choice, from a reward menu, for every 30-minute period in which he does not engage in physical aggression. It is important to note that rewards are not the same as bribes. In order to earn a reward, a student must first meet an expectation—in this case, going a set length of time without acting in an aggressive manner toward any other students. If Billy does not meet the expectation during any time period, he will not earn a reward.

As you work through this chapter, I challenge you to think about intentionality in teaching and learning. As an action researcher, this is what you are doing—making intentional decisions about the learning of your students. You are using individual student (or classroom) data, as well as peer-reviewed research, to determine appropriate interventions that address students' learning and behavior challenges. And, then you are diligently implementing those interventions and continually collecting data to ensure that students are making expected progress (either increased academic learning or decreased challenging behaviors or both).

After reading chapter 3, you hopefully have a better understanding of how to select an intervention that may support the learning or behavior needs of your students. And, by now, I assume that you have collected data, written a problem statement, and identified an intervention that you plan to implement for one student or a group of students in your own classroom or school.

I think this is a good time to remind you of the action research process. The process was introduced in chapter 1 and includes six steps. You can see a visual representation of the steps in figure 4.1. (Please note that this is the same flowchart found in chapter 1.)

Now that you have completed the first three steps in the action research process, let's talk about the next steps. After you choose the intervention, you must use that intervention to support your student's needs. But, first, you need to create a plan for how you will implement it and how you will evaluate whether it is working.

Identify a problem

⇩

Collect baseline data

⇩

Research evidence-based intervention

⇩

Select and implement an appropriate intervention

⇩

Collect data to determine the effectiveness of the intervention

⇩

Make adjustments to intervention plan to meet student needs

FIGURE 4.1.   Flowchart of Special Education Action Research Process

PLANNING FOR THE INTERVENTION

Benjamin Franklin once famously said, "If you fail to plan, you are planning to fail." This is true for many aspects of life, but especially for teachers in the special education classroom. Success for our students requires us to have solid plans for both the short term and the long term. We create daily lesson plans, quarterly unit plans, and grade-level scope and sequences. For individual students, we team with others to create Individualized Education Programs (IEPs) that articulate the specific plans we are making to ensure that child's success. These plans include goals, as well as the supports students require in order to achieve those goals. Without each of these plans, we would be less successful in supporting students. Similarly, we must make a solid plan for any intervention that we intend to use to support our students. Our plan must include

---

TEXTBOX 4.1
CONSIDERATIONS FOR INTERVENTION PLAN

How will the plan be implemented?
- When will the intervention occur? (Think about time of day, length of time, etc.)
- Who will implement the intervention?
- Who will implement the intervention when I am absent?
- How does the plan align with what the research says about the intervention (the plan should look similar to how the intervention is implemented in research studies)?

What tools and supports do I need?
- What training is needed to implement this intervention?
- What supplies/materials are needed? How will these be acquired?
- If the materials needed have a financial cost, what is the process for getting the necessary funds? Who will be in charge of obtaining the funds?
- What support is needed to ensure other job responsibilities do not prevent me from implementing the intervention?

How will the intervention success be evaluated?
- How will formative, ongoing data be collected?
- How often will data be collected?
- Who will collect data?
- Who will analyze the data?

What will I do next?
- After looking at the data, what will I do next? What intervention might we try next if the data indicates that this intervention is ineffective?

What else should I consider?

---

information about how we will implement the intervention, where we will acquire the needed supports, how we will evaluate our intervention success, and next steps. Textbox 4.1 offers a list of considerations when designing an intervention plan.

As you look at textbox 4.1, it is a lot of information to consider. To help you think through how to answer each of these considerations, textbox 4.2 offers an example of how Mr. Bullock might complete this form for Billy.

TEXTBOX 4.2
SAMPLE COMPLETED CONSIDERATIONS FOR INTERVENTION PLAN

How will the plan be implemented?
- When will the intervention occur? (Think about time of day, length of time, etc.)

  The intervention will be in effect for all hours of the school day, from the time that Billy arrives at school until he leaves.
- Who will implement the intervention?

  Mrs. Sanchez (a classroom paraprofessional) will have primary responsibility for implementing the intervention. When she is on break/lunch. Mr. Bullock will be responsible for implementing the intervention.
- Who will implement the intervention when I am absent?

  If Mr. Bullock is absent, Mrs. Sanchez will continue to implement the intervention and will be responsible for collecting any data. While Mrs. Sanchez is on break, Mr. Cho (another classroom paraprofessional) will implement the intervention.

  If Mrs. Sanchez is absent, Mr. Cho will implement the intervention, with the support of Mr. Bullock.
- How does the plan align with what the research says about the intervention (the plan should look similar to how the intervention is implemented in research studies)

  As a team, Mr. Bullock and his paraprofessionals have looked extensively at the research about both proximity control and rewards for students with emotional disturbance. The plan they have designed closely reflects the implementation plans from the research studies they have read. To ensure they are using best practices, each stakeholder has received a copy of the IRIS Center Fundamental Skill Sheets for proximity control, as well as a sheet of tips on using rewards that was created by their state department of education.

What tools and supports do I need?
- What training is needed to implement this intervention?

  Both Mrs. Sanchez and Mr. Cho will need training on how to use proximity control. Mr. Bullock will provide this training and will create a handout with the steps for implementation. The handout will be posted behind Mr. Bullock's desk so that all stakeholders can look at it when a reminder of the implementation process is needed.

In addition, both paraprofessionals should receive a reminder about how to use rewards in the classroom.

- What supplies/materials are needed? How will these be acquired?

The first supply needed is the handout, which Mr. Bullock will create, laminate, and post behind his desk. The other required supplies are the rewards that will be offered to Billy. Mr. Bullock is responsible for getting these rewards and ensuring that the treasure box always has options.

- If the materials needed have a financial cost, what is the process for getting the necessary funds? Who will be in charge of obtaining the funds?

The rewards offered to Billy may have a financial cost. Mr. Bullock is planning to focus primarily on free rewards, such as iPad time or jumping on the trampoline, but small tangible rewards may be needed. Mr. Bullock has a small classroom supplies budget ($50 per school year) and allocates half of the budget to purchasing small prizes for his classroom treasure box. He plans to use prizes from the treasure box as reward options. In addition, Mr. Bullock is going to ask Billy's parents to donate some prizes. Because they are seeing the same aggression toward his brother at home and are concerned about safety, Billy's parents want to support the school in addressing the behavior.

- What support is needed to ensure other job responsibilities do not prevent me from implementing the intervention?

Using proximity control is going to require significant time from Mrs. Sanchez and will make it harder for her to support other learners in the classroom. During the initial phase of the intervention, it will be important to ensure that other students will need minimal assistance with their work. With this in mind, Mr. Bullock plans to use more computer-directed learning activities and whole-class activities, as well as do a weeklong review unit in math.

How will the intervention success be evaluated?

- How will formative, ongoing data be collected?

Observational data will be collected. Mrs. Sanchez will take ABC data whenever Billy is frustrated. In addition, when/if Billy exhibits physical aggression, the following data will be collected: a description of the behavior, an estimate of the length of the aggressive incident, an explanation of the consequence, and Billy's description of why he engaged in aggressive behavior.

- How often will data be collected?

Data will be collected on a daily basis and more thorough data will be collected when/if an aggressive incident occurs.

- Who will collect data?

Mrs. Sanchez will have primary responsibility to data collection. However, when aggressive incidents occur, any adult who witnessed the event will be asked to provide a written description of what they observed.

- Who will analyze the data?

Mr. Bullock and Mrs. Sanchez will analyze the data together.

What will I do next?

- After looking at the data, what will I do next? What intervention might we try next if the data indicates that this intervention is ineffective?

  If proximity control appears to be working, we will create a plan to ensure that Billy is always near an adult. However, we cannot continue this existing plan for the long term as we don't have the staff to have an adult dedicated to staying with Billy at all times. In addition, we want to phase out this intervention, so once Billy is no longer being aggressive toward his brother, we will lengthen the time between rewards.

  If the intervention is not effective, or not as effective as we would like, we will try two interventions: social skills instruction that includes role playing of appropriate responses to frustration and offering frequent breaks, especially when Billy is frustrated. If these interventions are also not as effective as we hope, we will contact the school district behavior specialist for additional support.

What else should I consider?

Because Billy will be receiving rewards, his classmates might feel jealous that they are not getting rewards. This may be especially true for Billy's brother. We will need to work with their parents to ensure that both boys' needs are being met. In addition, we may want to give daily class wide rewards, such as five-minute recess time at the end of the day, to encourage all students to keep meeting learning expectations.

The implementation of this intervention is going to be a lot of work for Mrs. Sanchez. Mr. Bullock will need to check in our her frequently to see what support she needs. He may want to consider having Mr. Cho implement the intervention one day per week so that Mrs. Sanchez has a break.

If the intervention is needed for a long period of time, the academic learning of the other students in the classroom may be impacted. Review activities, group work, and computer-based learning are not designed to meet each students' individual needs.

Billy's IEP identifies that he has an emotional disturbance. His aggressive behavior may be a manifestation of his disability. This means that it may take longer than expected to address this challenge and we may need to gain the support of other special education professionals within the school district in order to ensure that we are providing him the most appropriate supports.

As you look at the list of considerations, you will notice that it is very long. As much as possible, you should consider problems or needs that might arise, as well as the impact of the intervention on other students and on adults in the classroom. No student learns in isolation, and anything that occurs in the classroom will have some impact on all other students in the classroom. While you cannot predict every challenge that may come up, if you have planned for the likely ones, your intervention will be smoother and have less of an impact on your classroom. In addition, you may notice that this considerations form includes a plan to seek assistance from the district behavior specialist, if needed. It is important to remember that you are not expected to know everything and you should ask for help when needed. Effective instruction for students with disabilities is a team effort! Finally, the last statement on the form is a reminder that Billy has a disability and this challenging behavior is likely a manifestation of that disability.

After you have designed your plan, you need to share it with all relevant stakeholders. Depending on your school and the specific intervention being implemented, the list of stakeholders might include (a) general education teachers, (b) paraprofessionals, (c) related service providers, (d) school or district administration, (e) parents, and (f) other relevant parties. The more complex the intervention, the more stakeholders that may need to be involved. If components of the intervention will be implemented outside of your classroom (for example, the general education classroom, the hallway, the lunchroom, the music classroom, etc.), you will need to share the plan with the teachers and other school staff members who work in these environments. If the intervention requires the support of other stakeholders in the school (such as the school counselor to provide counseling sessions), you will need to ensure that they are willing and able to offer that support. Whenever possible or appropriate, you will want to include these individual stakeholders in the planning process as you design the intervention.

IRB APPLICATIONS AND APPROVAL

If you are conducting your action research with plans to publish or present your findings (or if your university requires you to do so), IRB approval may be necessary. IRB is the acronym commonly used to refer to the Institutional Review Board. These organizations are tasked with reviewing research studies that university faculty or students plan to conduct. Under federal law, your university IRB has the authority to approve your research study, ask for modifications to your research plan, or deny approval for the research that you plan to conduct (U.S. Department of Education, 2011). The primary responsibility of the IRB is to ensure that any research that is being conducted is safe for "human subjects," which is the term used to refer to participants in a study. Keep in mind that, as the researcher, you are not one of these participants. The participants being protected are the students or adults that you are studying.

The U.S. Department of Health and Human Services (2020) provides a flowchart that helps researchers and universities decide if a specific project requires IRB approval. This flowchart indicates that action research that is considered part of normal educational practices does not need IRB approval. This means that if you are a classroom teacher and are doing action research as a normal part of your classroom instruction, you do not need IRB approval. With that being said, your professor or your university may still require you to get approval. To look at the flowchart, check out this link on the HHS website: https://www.hhs.gov/ohrp/regulations-and-policy/decision-charts-2018/index.html.

While every university's IRB form will look a bit different, there are some common components that are generally requested in this document. Textbox 4.3 offers a checklist of information that you will need to have before completing the IRB form—keep in mind, though, that your university may require additional

---

TEXTBOX 4.3
INFORMATION NEEDED TO COMPLETE IRB APPLICATION

- **Your personal information:** name, degree you are seeking, email address, phone number
- **Title of the project:** This does not need to be anything fancy and is likely not the title that you will give the manuscript you write based on the research. Instead, this is a simple title that explains what you plan to research.
- **Timeline for the project:** What date do you plan to begin the research and by what date will your research end?
- **Research team:** This is you and any colleagues (inside or outside of your university) who are collaborating with you on the action research
- **Literature review:** This is not a thorough review of the literature, but instead is a paragraph or two that describes previous research on the topic. Be sure to include in-text citations and references.
- **Research methodology:** This is an explicit explanation of the research that you plan to conduct. For this section, I recommend a numbered list so that it is easy for the IRB to understand your plan
- **Description of participants:** This section describes who will be the focus of your study. Include the number of participants and any other relevant information. The IRB will likely explicitly ask if they are minors, if they have disabilities, and if anyone involved is pregnant.
- **Plans for gaining consent:** You will need to have consent from all participants before beginning a research study, and the IRB will want to know those plans. If the study participants are minors, you will likely need consent from their parents and assent from the children.
- **Plans for ensuring confidentiality:** You will need to describe how you will keep the data confidential and where you will store that data after you collect it
- **Supplementary materials:** You will be asked to include any supplementary materials that will be used in the research. This might include (a) letters asking people to participate in the research study, (b) participant consent forms, and (c) surveys or questionnaires that you plan to use.
- **Signature:** You will likely need a signature from the school administrator of the location where your research will be conducted. In addition, your professor will need to sign to indicate their approval of your research plan.

information or may want the information formatted slightly differently than I have described below.

In order to help you conceptualize what your IRB form may include, textbox 4.4 offers a sample of a completed IRB form that Mr. Bullock might submit in his efforts to support Billy. However, keep in mind that your specific university may ask slightly different questions, want the information formatted differently, or ask for additional information. This textbox is simply one example of what you might be asked to submit. If you will need IRB approval for your action research project, I highly recommend finding samples of projects that have previously been approved by your university IRB and modeling your application on those documents.

Depending on your university, the IRB application process may take a long time, sometimes as long as three or four months, especially if multiple rounds of revisions are required. When you are planning your research study, it is important that you plan for this time. You might get lucky and get approval quickly, but it is better to expect a long process and get pleasantly surprised by a shorter wait.

TEXTBOX 4.4
SAMPLE IRB FORM FOR MR. BULLOCK

Imaginary IRB Application Form

Name: Joseph Bullock
Email address: Bullock@imaginaryuniversity.edu
Phone number: 555-123-4567
Program: Department of Special Education
Research project title: The impacts of using proximity control and rewards for reducing a student's challenging behaviors
Research project dates: January 15, 2022, to April 15, 2022
Additional research team members: Suzie Research, PhD

Abstract/literature review:
The U.S. Department of Education Office of Special Education Programs (2020) reports that more than 5% of K–12 students have been diagnosed with an emotional disturbance. Children who qualify for special education services in this category have a variety of needs that may include one or more of the following: (a) learning delays, (b) trouble building relationships, (c) inappropriate behaviors or feelings, (d) depression, and (e) physical symptoms (Council for Exceptional Children, 2022). Some students may engage in aggressive behaviors that include self-harm or harming others. A variety of interventions have proven to be effective for reducing these challenging behaviors. One evidence-based intervention is proximity control; this intervention involves a teacher or other classroom adult staying near the student during times when problem behaviors are likely to occur (Weaver et al., 2020). In addition, the use of rewards to incentivize continued appropriate

---

behavior is effective for reducing challenging behaviors and increasing undesired classroom behaviors (Simonsen et al., 2008). The proposed study aims to investigate the impact of using both proximity control and rewards to reduce the physically aggressive behaviors of a second-grade student who qualifies for special education serves as a student with an emotional disturbance.

References

Council for Exceptional Children. (2022). *Behavior disorders: Definitions, characteristics and related information.* https://debh.exceptionalchildren.org/behavior-disorders-definitions-characteristics-related-information

Simonsen, B., Fairbanks, S., Briesch, A., Myers, D., & Sugai, G. (2008). Evidence-based practices in classroom management: Considerations for research to practice. *Education and Treatment of Children, 31*(3), 351–80. https://psycnet.apa.org/doi/10.1353/etc.0.0007

U.S. Department of Education Office of Special Education Programs. (2020). *OSEP releases fast facts: Children identified with emotional disturbance.* https://sites.ed.gov/osers/2020/05/osep-releases-fast-facts-children-identified-with-emotional-disturbance/#:~:text=Data%20showed%20that%205.45%25%20of,disabilities%20identified%20with%20emotional%20disturbance.

Weaver, A. D., Scherer, P., Hengen, S., & Shriver, M. D. (2020). An exploratory investigation of proximity control in a large-group unstructured setting. *Preventing School Failure, 64*(3), 261–70. https://doi.org/10.1080/1045988X.2020.1747383

Research methodology:

1. Parents will be provided with information about the research study and asked to provide consent. If parents decline consent to participation in research, student will still be provided with intervention, but the results will only be used for instructional purposes and not for research purposes.
2. Student will be asked to provide verbal assent.
3. Classroom paraprofessionals will be provided training on the intervention.
4. The classroom paraprofessional will be responsible for providing proximity control from the time the student arrives at school each day until he leaves. This will require the paraprofessional staying within five feet of the student at all times.
5. If the student begins to engage in physically or verbally aggressive behaviors, the paraprofessional will place herself between the research participant and other students.
6. After every 10-minute period in which the student does not initiate physically or verbally aggressive behaviors, the student will receive a reward of his choice. The reward will be given to the student by the paraprofessional.
7. The time period between rewards will slowly increase as appropriate, based on the student's behaviors during the course of the action research study. The time period between rewards will be no longer than one hour.
8. Frequency count data (on the number of aggressive behaviors), as well observational data will be collected by the researcher, the classroom

paraprofessional, and other adult classroom stakeholders. This data will be compared to the baseline data that has been collected.

Description of participants:
The proposed research study involves one participant: a second-grade boy who has been identified as having an emotional disturbance and receives special education services. The researcher is the case manager and primary teacher for the research participant.

Plans for consent:
The student's parents will be provided information about the research study, as well as a consent form (located at the end of this proposal). After the parents provide consent, the researcher will explain the study to the student and ask for verbal assent. The researcher will answer any questions from the student and his parents that arise before, during, and after the research has been conducted.

Plans for confidentiality:
All data will be stored on a password protected file on the primary investigator's computer. Data will only be shared with the IEP team and other relevant stakeholders as needed to ensure appropriate educational outcomes.

Potential benefits and risks:
This action research may decrease the student's challenging behaviors and increase his academic success.
There are no foreseeable risks to this action research study.

Supplementary materials:
Consent Form
Dear Parent,
My name is Joseph Bullock and I am your child's special education teacher and case manager. I am currently pursuing my master's degree in special education at Imaginary University. As a requirement for the completion of my degree, I am completing a research study examining the impact of proximity control and rewards on aggressive behaviors. Proximity control occurs when a teacher or paraprofessional remains within a few feet of a student throughout the school day. Rewards will be provided to your child when he meets the classroom expectation of no physical aggression for a set period of time, beginning with ten-minute time periods and slowly increasing to an hour between each reward. Because the IEP team believes that these interventions will support your child, we will be trialing them in the classroom this spring. If you provide consent, the data we collect will be used to complete my master's degree action research project.

Participation in this research is voluntary and you may choose to decline to allow your child to participate. You also may withdraw your consent at any time.

To provide consent or decline to consent, please sign and return the form below.

IMPLEMENTING THE INTERVENTION

In chapter 3, there was a table (table 3.1) that offered a list of common learning and behavior challenges, as well as evidence-based interventions for addressing the challenges. Each of those interventions has research evidence to support the likelihood that it will be effective for supporting learners if its implementation is appropriately planned. Table 4.1 offers a basic plan for the implementation of two of those interventions. Keep in mind that the specific plan you create will be individualized to the student's needs, as well as the resources available within your school setting. But, even with the individualization, your plan should reflect accurate implementation of the EBP. You may notice as you read the plans in table 4.1 that the person responsible for every action is clearly named in each step of the plan. While this may seem a bit repetitive, it is important for ensuring that all stakeholders know who is responsible for each aspect of the plan. In addition, the plan includes steps for evaluating the effectiveness of the intervention. We will talk more about this process in chapter 5, but you should begin thinking about it now.

IMPLEMENTATION FIDELITY

Once the planning is complete, all stakeholders are on board with the plan, and you have received IRB approval if needed, it is time to get started! When implementing the intervention, it is vital that you follow the plan exactly. One of the listed considerations in figure 4.1 is how the plan aligns with research studies. Putting an intervention into practice exactly as designed is known as implementation fidelity. If we are not implementing an intervention in the way that it was designed and in the manner (or a similar manner) to how it has been researched, it is not an evidence-based intervention.

Breitenstein and colleagues (2010) note that interventions that are not implemented as designed may not lead to the desired results and may lead to stakeholders believing that an intervention is ineffective. They also note that

TABLE 4.1. Intervention implementation plans

Evidence-based practice	Intervention plan
Rewards for sitting at the table and working	1. The teacher will create a reward menu, which will include rewards Johnny is likely to want and that are readily available in the classroom.
	2. Before each table activity, Johnny will select the reward he will work to earn.
	3. During the activity, the teacher or paraprofessional will monitor Johnny to ensure that he is working on the assigned task at the table.
	4. If needed, the teacher or paraprofessional will remind Johnny of the expectations. No more than three reminders per activity will be provided.
	5. At the end of the activity, the teacher or paraprofessional will verbally tell Johnny whether he met the expectation of sitting at the table and working. If he met the expectation, the teacher or paraprofessional will give Johnny his selected reward. If Johnny did not meet the expectations, he will not receive the reward and the teacher or paraprofessional will verbally tell him why he did not meet the expectation.
	6. At the end of each school day, the teacher will send an email to Johnny's parents to indicate how many rewards he earned, as well as the number of activities in which he did not meet expectations.
	7. Each week, stakeholders will evaluate the effectiveness of the plan and make changes to the plan as needed.

(continued)

TABLE 4.1. *(continued)*

Evidence-based practice	Intervention plan
Listening to passage read aloud paired with repeated readings	1. The teacher will identify all texts that will be read by the class. Each text will be marked as a book that will be read aloud by the teacher or a book that students are responsible for reading independently.
	2. For each text that students must read independently, the teacher will locate an audio recording. If no audio recording exists, the teacher or paraprofessional will read the book aloud and record themselves reading.
	3. When students are required to read a text independently, Rafael will be provided with a copy of the text, the audio recording, and headphones. When the teacher is going to read the text aloud to the class, Rafael will be provided with a copy of the text.
	4. Rafael will listen to the text being read on the recording (or by the teacher) and follow along in his own copy of the book.
	5. After listening to the text being read aloud, Rafael will read the text two more times independently. If there is not time in class to complete these readings, Rafael will take the book home and read it there; when this happens, his parents are responsible for ensuring that he completes each reading.
	6. Rafael's understanding of the text will be assessed through classroom comprehension activities, such as class discussions and assignments.
	7. Rafael's reading comprehension will be evaluated at least weekly through a DIBELS probe and progress will be reported to all stakeholders every other Friday.
	8. After four weeks of intervention implementation, the team will determine whether to continue the intervention or select a new intervention.

common barriers to implementation fidelity include lack of training on implementation, insufficient resources needed to implement, or too many demands on a practitioner's time. If you look back at textbox 4.1, you will notice that your planning process specifically addresses each of these barriers, but that does not mean that you won't still face challenges in putting your plan into practice. Be prepared for these challenges so you can face them head-on when they arise! Textbox 4.5 offers a list of fantastic resources for learning more about how to implement educational interventions with fidelity.

CONCLUSION

At this point, you are well on your way to completing your action research project. You are now ready for the fun part—implementing the intervention! This is the point in your action research where you get to use what you know about effective instruction to support your student. Now is the time to utilize the EBPs that you have learned about in your previous courses. As you begin this part of your action research, there are a few things that I want you to keep in mind:

- Interventions often take time in order to lead to results. Please don't get frustrated if you don't see the results you want immediately.
- Implementation fidelity is critical. You must be consistent with how you are using the intervention. Even on the most challenging days, you must follow the exact plan that you created. If you don't, you will jeopardize the success of your action research.
- Action research is hard! It will be challenging for you and for any other stakeholders, including your paraprofessionals. Be sure to check in with them on a regular basis to see what support they need.
- Don't be afraid to ask for help from colleagues or other school district personnel, such as special education intervention specialists or administrators.

Teaching is not meant to be done alone. The most effective instruction and intervention occurs through a team-based approach.

- Remind yourself on a daily basis why you are doing this work. Look at the problem statement you created frequently and think about the positive impact this intervention may have on your student and your classroom.
- Your students are very lucky to have a teacher who wants to do their best to support student success. Remember that you are awesome and you are making an important impact on the world through your role as a special educator.

REVIEW QUESTIONS AND EXERCISES

1. In what ways does intentional planning and decision making apply to the concept of action research? Share what you think it means to seek learning with ardor? How will you, as a special education teacher, do this?

2. Textbox 4.1 provides a list of considerations for intervention planning. Consider your planned action research project and answer each of the questions from textbox 4.1 for the intervention that you plan to implement.

3. Table 4.1 offered two sample step-by-step intervention plans. Using these plans as a guide, create the intervention plan for your action research project.

4. Using the intervention plan you created in activity 3, design a one-page overview of the plan that you can share with stakeholders (parents, paraprofessionals, other school personnel).

5. If your university requires you to submit an IRB research study application for this action research project, complete that task, using the approved university form.

6. In this chapter, you learned about the concept of "implementation fidelity." Why is it important to implement interventions as designed? What might be the consequences in your school if interventions are not implemented with fidelity? Consider your "elevator speech" for how you will explain this concept to your colleagues.

Evaluating the Effectiveness of the Intervention

....

Student Learning Objectives

After reading chapter 5 and completing the exercises at the end of the chapter, students will be able to do the following:

- Define the term "formative evaluation" and articulate its role in the action research process
- Describe various formative evaluation methods that can be used in action research
- Plan and use an appropriate formative evaluation process for their action research project
- Use the formative data to determine the effectiveness of an intervention

Mr. Bullock and his paraprofessionals have identified the interventions that they want to try using in order to support Billy's behavior needs. Based on their baseline data, they have determined that the best evidence-based practices (EBPs) to implement are proximity control and rewards for meeting behavior expectations. They have completed all steps in the intervention planning process and have received Institutional Review Board (IRB) approval for the research. Mr. Bullock has shared his plan with the other Individualized Education Program (IEP) team members and received permission from Billy's parents to use this intervention for his master's degree action research project. Each stakeholder feels prepared for addressing any challenges that may arise while implementing the intervention. On Monday morning, the team begins implementation of the selected interventions and takes ongoing data to understand whether their plan is working.

In chapter 4, we talked about implementing your intervention to determine its effectiveness for support the learning or behavior needs of your students. As an action researcher, I like to think of myself as

....

a detective. I pretend that I am Nancy Drew, but you could be one of the Hardy Boys or Sherlock Holmes. My children would likely pretend to be Cam Jansen or Encyclopedia Brown. It doesn't matter which detective you emulate as long as you focus on the role of looking for clues (in the form of data) that will help you to help your students. Just like when our favorite detectives are solving mysteries, we need data to come up with theories (or problem statements) in action research and the data we collect guides our instruction and intervention. As you prepared for implementing your action research project, you collected data that provided you with a hypothesis about the student's needs. You used that hypothesis to select an evidence-based practice for your intervention and have likely begun implementing that intervention. Just like good data was important in the planning stage of your action research, it is also vital during implementation. The data gives us evidence as to whether our selected intervention really is appropriate for the needs of the student. In this chapter, we will talk about using data to understand the effectiveness of the intervention you are implementing.

FORMATIVE EVALUATION

As you are implementing your intervention, you will need to gather data on a regular basis. Data that is collected during the learning process is referred to as formative data (Cornelius, 2013). This should not be confused with summative evaluation data, which is the data you collect at the end of a learning unit or intervention (Dixson & Worrell, 2016). Both forms of data are important in understanding the impact of an intervention. But you cannot wait until your intervention is completed or until you have been using the intervention for several weeks to start collecting data. Data collection is an ongoing process that guides teaching practices.

The formative data you collect and the data collection method you use will be similar to the data collection you completed in chapter 2, when you gathered baseline data. In that chapter, we discussed the importance of collecting data from a variety of sources, so you likely used more than one data-collection method. When you are planning for formative data collection, I recommend using one or more of the same methods you used during baseline data collection. You do not need to use every method for formative data collection; simply choose the method(s) that are most appropriate to your needs. As a reminder, we talked about various data collection methods in chapter 2, including: (a) assessments, (b) work samples, (c) observations, (d) interviews, (e) surveys, (f) checklists, and (g) rating scales. Table 5.1 offers a brief reminder of each of these data-collection methods, as well as an example of how each of these methods may be used as formative assessment tools.

As you think about which formative data-collection method to use, be sure to consider the practicality of using that method on a regular basis. For example,

TABLE 5.1.   Data collection methods for assessing intervention effectiveness

Data collection method	Overview of method	Example of use for formative assessment
Assessments	• Standardized: student score can be compared to the scores of others • May include quizzes from the curriculum • Curriculum-based measurements are common form of assessment	Mr. Seuss administers a DIBELS fluency probe to the second-grade reading intervention students every Thursday. He charts the students' scores over time to better understand their progress.
Work Samples	• Class assignments, exit tickets, or homework • Using rubrics to evaluate work samples can lead to more useable data	Ms. Bali uses a writing rubric to evaluate the weekly paragraph assignment in her class. The rubric is specifically designed to evaluate the skills needed for success in sixth-grade writing, including the use of an introduction and conclusion, a thesis statement, organization, supporting details and mechanics. Ms. Bali uses the same rubric each week so that she can evaluate student's writing progress.
Observations	• Written document of behavior • Includes information about what happened before and after behavior • Information included must be explicit • Should be based on the facts, not opinions or guesses about motivation	Johnny's teacher used a table to write observation notes about his behaviors of kicking the table and screaming. The baseline data indicated that Johnny may engage in these behaviors when he is frustrated.
Interviews	• May be structured, semistructured, or unstructured • Various stakeholders may be interviewed • Can be time consuming	Mrs. Roberts is collecting formative data on Sam's use of inappropriate language on the playground. Every day, Mrs. Roberts asks one classmate who was near Sam during recess whether they overheard any inappropriate language. Mrs. Roberts varies the classmate she interviews and keeps track of their responses.

(continued)

TABLE 5.1. *(continued)*

Data collection method	Overview of method	Example of use for formative assessment
Surveys	• Can be used to gain information from a large group of people • Wording of questions is critical • Questions may be open ended or closed ended	Mr. Agosti is the special education director for a school district. For this school year, he has designed a monthly professional development series for all teachers in the district on the Universal Design for Learning (UDL) framework. He wants to evaluate the impact of each session so that he can make adjustments for future learning. After each monthly professional development, Mr. Agosti sends an anonymous survey to all teachers who attended the session. The survey includes a combination of open-ended and closed-ended questions about the session itself, teachers' self-reported use of UDL in their classrooms, and the needs of teachers in implementing what they are learning. After receiving the surveys each month, Mr. Agosti adjusts upcoming professional development sessions to ensure that teachers' needs are met.
Checklists	• A list of skills that students must master • Teacher indicates whether the student has mastered each skill • Data is more accurate when multiple stakeholders complete the checklist for a student	Asha is a high school student who frequently arrives at class unprepared for learning. She often does not have her homework, textbook, paper, or pencil. Asha's special education case manager is using a visual prompt in Asha's locker to support her success but needs to evaluate the impact of this intervention. The case manager has created a checklist that she asks each of Asha's teachers to complete each day. The checklist includes four skills and for each skill, the option is yes or no: 1. Asha brought her homework to class. 2. Asha brought her textbook to class. 3. Asha brought paper to class. 4. Asha brought a writing utensil to class.

Data collection method	Overview of method	Example of use for formative assessment
Rating scales	• A list of skills that students must master • Teacher indicates the extent to which the student has mastered each skill • Data is more accurate when multiple stakeholders complete the checklist for a student	Ralphie is working on learning the steps for the morning classroom routine, which includes putting his backpack/coat in his locker, getting his work folder, and working independently at his desk. There are a total of 20 discrete steps in this routine and Ralphie's teacher has designed a checklist to evaluate the extent to which Ralphie can complete each step. The checklist tracks the skills he can complete independently, with visual prompts, with verbal prompts, with both visual and verbal prompts, and the skills he is unable to complete. Two mornings each week, the classroom paraprofessional observes Ralphie during the morning routine and fills out the checklist.

it is not practical to conduct a weekly interview with a student's parents to evaluate the effectiveness of an intervention. Instead, you could do a weekly phone call to see their thoughts or have them complete a short checklist each week. You could pair that data with observational data or work sample data that you are collecting in the classroom. Be sure to select a formative evaluation method that is appropriate for both the student need and the realities of the classroom.

ANALYZING THE FORMATIVE DATA

Once you have selected the data collection method (or methods) you will use, you need to consider how you will analyze that data. In the most basic explanation, what you are looking for in your data is a trend in the correct direction. For example, Mr. Bullock in the vignette is looking for data that indicates that Billy's aggressive behaviors are occurring less frequently or are less aggressive over time. Mr. Seuss from table 5.1 is looking for an increase in reading fluency. He is asking the question of whether students are reading more words per minute each week.

In this rest of this section, we will consider these two classroom scenarios with examples of data that might be collected for both Billy and for Mr. Seuss' students. Table 5.2 offers one week's worth of sample formative observational data about Billy, while table 5.3 is a chart of DIBELS (*Dynamic Indicators of Basic*

TABLE 5.2. Formative observational data for Billy

Date	Observation notes	Number of rewards received (15 possible)	Additional comments
October 1	Billy tried to kick his brother on 8 different occasions during the day. Because Mrs. Sanchez was near Billy, she was able to get between Billy and his brother. In six of the instances, her presence made Billy stop mid-kick and scream, "Ahh!" instead of kicking. In two of the occurrences, Billy did not stop and Mrs. Sanchez got kicked in the shin. Each time that Billy tried to kick his brother, the 30-minute clock was reset.	9/15	First day of intervention implementation Mrs. Sanchez reports concern that she cannot be kicked every day as she now has a bruise on her leg.
October 2	Billy tried to kick his brother seven different times, all during the morning, but was not successful. When Mrs. Sanchez was kicked once. In the afternoon, Billy made a growling sound and bared his teeth at his brother five times but did not attempt to kick him.	11/15	For the purposes of rewards, growling was not considered as physical aggression, so Billy was able to earn rewards in the afternoon.
October 3	Billy tried to kick his brother 20 times and was successful three times. He kicked Mrs. Sanchez 5 times. Each time that Billy attempted to kick (whether or not he was successful), he made a growling noise.	6/15	Note added on October 4: Billy was home sick with an ear infection the next day.
October 4	Billy was absent as he was home sick.		
October 5			Because Mrs. Sanchez had large bruises on both legs, she requested to have Mr. Cho implement the intervention. Mr. Bullock agreed. Billy is taking an antibiotic and was given Tylenol before school for his ear infection.

Early Literacy Skills) assessment scores for the second graders in Mr. Seuss' classroom.

This table offers an example of a formative data-collection process that is appropriate for many behavior-focused action research projects. As you look at the formative data about Billy, you may notice several things.

- The data being collected is not extensive. It likely only takes Mr. Bullock and Mrs. Sanchez about five minutes each day to complete the data collection form. Keeping the data collection as simple as possible, while still documenting the most important information, ensures that your formative data-collection method is sustainable over time.
- There does not seem to be a clear trend in the data. Because this is only one week's worth of data, that is not surprising. As mentioned previously in this book, it takes time to know whether an intervention works for a student.
- Billy was absent for one day. This is a common reality with action research. Action research focuses on real-life situations in the classroom, which means that things won't always go as planned. While you are implementing your action research, expect that children or adults may be unexpectedly absent, fire drills will occur, and schoolwide assemblies and field trips will be scheduled. This is normal life in a school. Just be sure to document these events as they may impact the intervention.
- On the third day, there is a note that Billy was sick the following day. Because illness can have an impact on behavior, this is important information to include.
- On the last day of data collection, the notes indicate that Mr. Bullock made a change to the plans and had Mr. Cho in charge of implementing the intervention instead of Mrs. Sanchez. Sometimes, it is appropriate to make unplanned adaptations to the intervention in order to support the needs of stakeholders. When we make these adaptations, though, it is vital that we note this and consider the impact the change may have on the intervention. For example, over time, Mr. Bullock needs to look at the data when Mr. Cho is implementing the intervention versus when Mrs. Sanchez implements it. He should evaluate whether the paraprofessional involved impacts Billy's behavior.

A simple observation form is a useful method for tracking behavior data, but it is not appropriate for all forms of formative data collection. When we consider Mr. Seuss' second graders' reading fluency, we would want to use a different data collection tool. In this situation, Mr. Seuss wants to understand the impact on reading fluency of the reading intervention he is using in his classroom. He is administering a second grade DIBELS reading fluency probe to each of the five students in the intervention group once per week and is

TABLE 5.3. Sample DIBELS reading fluency scores

Date	Student 1	Student 2	Student 3	Student 4	Student 5
January 6	41	19	47	43	39
January 13	42	10	50	45	40
January 20	43	19	54	47	40
January 27	44	21	60	48	41
February 3	45	20	63	50	41
February 10	46	19	70	53	41
February 17	47	17	72	55	42

looking for an upward trend in the number of words each student is reading correctly per minute. Table 5.3 shows a simple table that Mr. Seuss could use to track this data.

When looking at Table 5.3, a quick glance tells us that four of the five students appear to have a positive trend in their reading fluency scores and that Student 2's trend may be mostly stagnant. However, Mr. Seuss may want to look at this data through a visual representation. To do this, he can take the data collected on this form and graph it. Figure 5.1 shows a graph of the data.

After looking at both the table and the graph, Mr. Seuss sees that Students 1, 3, 4, and 5 have an upward trendline, indicating that their reading fluency rates are increasing. Student 2, on the other hand, has a mostly stagnant trendline. His reading fluency scores after seven weeks of intervention are similar to his scores at the beginning.

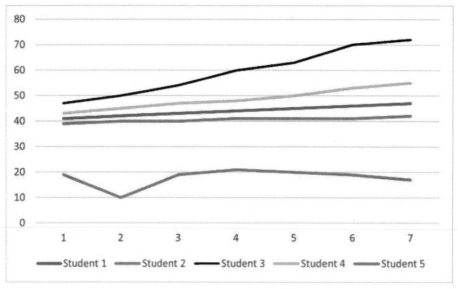

FIGURE 5.1. DIBELS Data for Mr. Seuss' Students

When you look at both table 5.3 and figure 5.1, there are a few points you should notice:

- Mr. Seuss is using the same form to collect data for all students. This is appropriate, and often the easiest method, when multiple students are working toward the same (or similar) goals.
- It can be beneficial to look at the same data in different formats. Seeing the class data in both table and graph form can help Mr. Seuss better understand the data.
- Student rates of progress may be drastically different, even with the same intervention. When you look at figure 5.1, you will see that Student 3's reading fluency is improving quickly, while Student 5 is making slower progress.
- For some students, additional data may need to be collected. For example, you may notice that Student 2 is not improving in their reading fluency. Mr. Seuss may need to collect more comprehensive data on this student's reading to better understand their needs.

DETERMINING EFFECTIVENESS OF INTERVENTION

After analyzing the data, you need to determine if your intervention is working as intended. As mentioned in the last section, you are trying to determine whether the data is showing the trend you want. When we look at the data from the previous section, we can learn a few things. First, the formative data regarding Billy's intervention is inconclusive. Based on one week of data, we are unable to know if proximity control and rewards are effective strategies for reducing Billy's kicking of his brother. We will need to collect data for at least a few more weeks before making any decisions.

When we look at the reading fluency data, we can see that the current intervention is not working for Student 2 and that Mr. Seuss needs to find a different EBP for supporting this student's needs. In reality, Mr. Seuss likely would have looked at the data in Week 4 or 5 and decided to try a new intervention for this student instead of continuing until Week 7. Mr. Seuss will go back to Steps 3 and 4 in the action research process in order to support this student. As a quick refresher, Step 3 is to research EBPs and Step 4 is to select an intervention to implement for the student. Because the group-wide intervention is not working for Student 2, Mr. Seuss will select an individualized EBP and implement it for this student without changing instruction for the other students. If you are currently working in a school that uses the Multi-Tiered System of Support (MTSS) framework, think of this example as Mr. Seuss using a Tier 2 intervention for his students. He finds that it works for most of them, but one student needs more and will receive a Tier 3 intervention.

When we look at the data for Mr. Seuss' other students, it looks like they are all making progress. However, in some cases, the direction of the trend does not tell the entire story. For some skills, we also must consider the rate with which change is occurring. While any progress is good, we sometimes need change to occur at a certain minimal rate. While Student 5 is showing an improvement in their reading fluency, that increase in words correct per minute is slow, with fewer than one additional word each week. When Mr. Seuss consults the DIBELS scoring guide, he sees that this increase does not meet the expected Zone of Growth that he should expect for a second-grade student. "The Zone of Growth" is a term used in the DIBELS assessment to indicate the expected rate of reading fluency progress for students (University of Oregon Center on Teaching and Learning, 2020). Because Student 5 is not making expected progress, Mr. Seuss will also need to go back to action research Steps 3 and 4 for this student. When doing this, he may select the same intervention he selected for Student 2 or he may select a different intervention. Remember that as special educators, our focus is on instruction and interventions that meet individual student needs. The EBPs we select for various students, even for the same needs, may differ.

SEEKING STAKEHOLDER INPUT WHEN LOOKING AT DATA

Effective teachers do not work alone. We can best support student learning and have the highest likelihood of ensuring student success when we team with others. For our special education students, we have a built-in team of stakeholders who are knowledgeable about the student and their needs. We should rely on the expertise of the members of the IEP team.

When sharing your data with others, you may find that each stakeholder understands or interprets that data differently. In one of the courses that I teach, I have all students watch a video of Swiper the Fox stealing from Dora and Boots and collect observational data. Then, I have the students discuss their data and create plans for addressing Swiper's behavior challenge. It never ceases to amaze me that each student's data is unique. The specific observations they make are different, and they have differing hypothesis on the function of the behavior, as well as how to reduce the challenging swiping behavior. Some students will take note of the exact words or actions that Dora uses before Swiper steals, while others will focus solely on Swiper's actions. Some students believe that Swiper steals to gain attention, while others believe he does so because he is hungry and Dora has food. Others hypothesize that he steals the items to sell them and uses that money to care for his family. Because students have differing ideas of why Swiper steals from Dora and Boots, they select a variety of evidence-based practices for reducing the behavior.

Just like my students have different interpretations of Swiper's behavior, you and your colleagues will likely have various thoughts about the data you have collected regarding your student's learning or behavior challenge. Each of our past experiences with students, as well as our individual experiences with the student receiving the intervention, will influence our understanding of the data. The National Research Council (2000) states that our brains depend upon our previous knowledge and experience to understand and interpret current events.

While it may be discouraging to consider that each stakeholder may interpret the data differently, this is actually one of the reasons that it is vital to discuss the data with colleagues. Together, you are more likely to construct a comprehensive understanding of the reality. When you each share what you think the data is saying, the other stakeholders may gain new insights into the situation. Consider the following example of an IEP team discussing student intervention data:

Special education teacher: Thanks for coming to this meeting, everyone. Earlier this week, I provided you all a copy of the baseline data we have collected regarding Emmanuel's verbal outbursts. I hope that you have had time to review it, but just in case you have not, I will offer a quick overview. Emmanuel's paraprofessional, Mr. Alvers, collected data over the course of two weeks and found that Emmanuel has an average of fourteen verbal outbursts each day and that the majority of these outbursts occur in the afternoon. I would love to hear each of your thoughts on this data and your own experiences with Emmanuel's outbursts in class.

Math teacher: Thank you for providing this data for us to review. I found it very useful and I compared it to the data that I collected in my classroom last week. Emmanuel is in my classroom immediately following his lunch period and had at least one outburst each day. On Monday, he screamed the "F" word when he encountered a challenging math problem. On Tuesday and Thursday, he yelled "No!" when I requested that the class complete an exit ticket before leaving the classroom. And, on both Wednesday and Friday, he had two outbursts when another student was using the protractor that he needed to complete this work.

History teacher: Well, I have no data of my own, but I have seen Emmanuel's outbursts a lot recently! It seems like every time that I ask him to do something, he yells about the request. Frankly, it is exhausting. I think he just does not like to work hard.

Special education teacher: Like you both, I have noticed that Emmanuel does seem to have outbursts when he is feeling frustrated, but it does not seem to be every time that he is upset. This morning, I saw him close his eyes and count to 10 before responding to a classmate who was speaking unkindly to him.

Science teacher: I agree. I have seen that Emmanuel can handle challenging situations well. I have lunch duty during his lunch period. Emmanuel always asks for the same food: a cheeseburger, applesauce, and chocolate milk. Sometimes, he is quite upset when one of those foods is not available, but at other times, he says "OK" and chooses a different meal. I cannot figure out why he responds differently on some days.

Language arts teacher: Wow! The data I reviewed before this meeting and everything you are all saying to me is shocking! I have not seen any of this. Emmanuel is always courteous and polite in my classroom. I cannot even imagine him saying the "F" word or having any kind of outburst.

Special education teacher: Hmmm, that is so interesting. I wonder why his behavior is so different in your classroom. Mr. Alvers, do you have any thoughts?

Mr. Alvers: This is all correct. Emmanuel has never had an outburst or any behavior concerns in language arts or in any of his specials. I cannot figure out why, though. I have seen him be frustrated by challenging work and by the actions of his classmates in each of those classrooms. So, I am not sure if frustration is the primary reason that Emmanuel has verbal outbursts.

Special education teacher: OK, if the outbursts are not caused by frustration, what could be causing them? Could it be frustration paired with something else? Thoughts? Ideas?

Science teacher: I have a question. Who had the protractor when he needed it during those math lessons? Is there any chance that it was Ralphie?

Math teacher: Let me think . . . actually, yes, now that you mention it, I believe it was Ralphie both times.

Science teacher: Ok, I have a hypothesis. I think the outbursts may be a response to Ralphie having something that Emmanuel wants. As I have been sitting here in this meeting, I thought about the times that he has had an outburst at lunch. Each time, Ralphie got the last of whatever food Emmanuel wanted.

History teacher: Now that I think about it, the outbursts do seem to happen after Ralphie says something about the work in my class being so easy.

Special education teacher: Wow! This is all so interesting and I had not even considered the ongoing friendship issues between Emmanuel and Ralphie. It is my understanding that they have been enemies since kindergarten and that their families also fight with one another. So, maybe the issue is related to Ralphie. I am not sure, though, what classes they have together.

Mr. Alvers: Actually, they are together the most in the afternoon, so that might explain the fact that the afternoon data shows more outbursts. Also, the classes where I have not witnessed any outbursts are the ones that Ralphie is not also in.

Special education teacher: So, what I am hearing is that Emmanuel has verbal outbursts most commonly when he is frustrated and Ralphie is nearby. Anyone have any further thoughts or insights?

History teacher: I know that these two boys are very competitive with one another, so this makes sense to me. Just this month, they were the top competitors for the school football team quarterback and trumpet section leader in band. Ralphie is the school's new quarterback and Emmanuel is the section leader. Obviously, the boys take several classes together and are in some of the same activities, so we can't keep them apart. What can we do to reduce the outbursts?

Special education teacher: Well, I have a few ideas, but I want to hear what you all think too.

This example was a very condensed version of the conversation that is likely to occur when stakeholders discuss data. In all reality, the conversations with your colleagues may take an hour or more as you compare what each person knows and come up with potential solutions together. As you read through that example, you may have noticed that each person had a slightly different idea. Some team members came to the meeting with information that others did not have. This information ended up being vital in understanding the situation. The team members shared their ideas and they all left the conversation with interpretations that differed, at least slightly, from the beginning of the conversation. They can use their shared interpretations to continue looking at the data so they can best support the needs of the student.

CONCLUSION

At this point, you have learned all the steps in the action research process. You have likely been conducting your own action research and are collecting data to understand the impact of the intervention plan you created in chapter 4. You will continue conducting that intervention and collecting data for several weeks. Keep an eye on the data you are collecting so that you can watch for trends. I recommend looking at the data in various formats, such as the table and graph for Mr. Seuss' students. Whenever possible, ask other stakeholders to help you analyze the data. Your classroom paraprofessional or general education teachers in your school may have insights into what the data means. If you need support or guidance in understanding your data, be sure to ask your professor or another teacher in your school.

REVIEW QUESTIONS AND EXERCISES

1. Write a one-paragraph explanation of formative evaluation and explain its role in the action research process. Be sure to consider the impact of using formative data, as well as the potential consequences of not doing so.

2. Table 5.1 offers a list of potential formative evaluation methods, as well as scenarios in which these methods may be used. Consider the learning and behavior needs of students in your classroom. For each method listed in table 5.1, identify a potential scenario in which you can use that data collection method to support the learning of your students.

3. Think about the action research project that you are implementing. Make a plan for how you will collect and analyze formative data.

4. As you collect data, create a chart or other tool that you can use to share your data with stakeholders. After you have created this tool, use it to share your data. Seek the feedback of stakeholders in better understanding what the data means. If your interpretations of the data differ, figure out what might be causing that difference.

5. Look at the data you have collected. Write a short description of what this data means for your student. Include information about what you have learned regarding the impact of this intervention for your student, as well as next steps.

CHAPTER 6

Sharing Your Research

....

Student Learning Objectives

After reading chapter 6 and completing the exercises at the end of the chapter, students will be able to do the following:

- Identify the importance of sharing action research
- Describe ways that they can disseminate their action research
- Plan how to share their action research project with the education community

Congratulations! You have concluded your action research study. Over the past several weeks, you have identified a need in your classroom, investigated evidence-based practices for addressing that need, selected an intervention, implemented that intervention, and collected data to determine the effectiveness of that intervention. You now know to what extent that specific intervention supports the needs of your student(s), and this is very useful knowledge that will help you to continue supporting the needs of your students. This is wonderful! But there is even more you can do! You can share what you have learned with other teachers. You must circulate what you learn in order to increase its value. To get the most benefit from the work you have done, you need to share what you have learned. If you simply keep your learning to yourself, it will benefit you and your students, but it will not help others around you. Additionally, if you are using this textbook as part of a course, it is likely that you will be required to share your research. So, let's talk about how to share your research and your learning, both formally and informally.

SHARING DATA WITH COLLEAGUES

Sharing your research with colleagues in your school is critical. When you share what you learn with other educators who also support your student, they can use what you learned to support that same student. Consider the case study of Pierre (see appendix A). Through the action research project, we learned that Pierre is more successful when we use a taped problems intervention to support his math fact fluency. We assume that his teacher, Mrs. Hathcote, will continue using the intervention. However, if that intervention is only used when Mrs. Hathcote provides instruction, Pierre's success will be limited. In order for Pierre to be successful in mathematics, every teacher should be using effective interventions. When Mrs. Hathcote shares her findings with colleagues, they will know that the intervention works for Pierre and can begin using it in their own classrooms. This intervention will likely support Pierre in his science classroom, as well as other educational settings.

In the school setting, there are a variety of ways that you can share what you learned with colleagues. One strategy is through meetings with each teacher that provides instruction to the student. These can be individual meetings with each teacher or a team meeting for all teachers who are responsible for instructing the student. A second option is through the written word, either an email or written note. Another idea is to record a video presentation in which you explain what you have learned. Keep in mind, though, that the use of a video may feel less personal than a meeting or a written note. Regardless of the format in which you share your research with colleagues, it is important that you offer the following information: (a) the baseline data, with an explanation of what the data means, (b) a thorough explanation of the intervention with practical examples of how each teacher can use the intervention in their own classroom setting, (c) solutions for addressing challenges that might arise in implementing the intervention, (d) information about where the teacher can locate any resources needed for implementation, and (e) a statement that you are willing to support the teacher as needed as they learn to use the intervention. After you have initially shared what you have learned, it is vital that you check in with your colleagues on occasion, especially if they are beginning to use what you have learned to support the same student. They may have questions or want to share their own success story with you.

As you think about how to share what you have learned with your colleagues, look at the letter below that Mr. Bullock (from the vignettes at the beginning of each chapter) wrote to his colleagues about Billy. You will note that the letter is addressed to one specific teacher and notes situations that have occurred in that classroom. Mr. Bullock used similar verbiage in each letter but made it more personal by writing a note to each teacher who provides instruction to Billy and presenting a solution to specific concerns that the teacher has noted.

Dear Ms. Smith,

I first want to thank you for working so hard to support students with disabilities in your classroom this school year. I have been very impressed by the successes that the students on my caseload have experienced due to your instruction. Today, I am particularly thankful for your patience and willingness to support Billy. I know that Billy's behaviors have been especially challenging over the past few months and have negatively impacted both his learning and the learning of his classmates. Last week, he attempted to kick his brother several times during your Music class, making it nearly impossible for you to teach the second graders how to play the recorder. As I shared with you, he has had similar behavior in my classroom.

Today, I want to share with you about an intervention I have been using in my classroom. I have been using both proximity control and rewards. This combination of interventions has reduced the challenging behaviors and has given our entire class more time for learning. I am attaching a copy of the behavior chart that I have been using to this email. In addition, I would love to talk to you about how I have implemented this intervention in my classroom.

Thank you again for your hard work in supporting Billy!

—Mr. Bullock

Once the action research is complete, the special education teacher should also share the data with the student's IEP team and should include intervention information in the IEP document as appropriate. IDEA requires special educators to use evidence-based practices for teaching and supporting learners with disabilities (Yell et al., 2017). When special educators conduct action research, they look at EBPs and test their effectiveness for individual student needs, ensuring that the practice is effective and appropriate for the learner and their learning environment (Russo-Campisi, 2017). By sharing what you learn through your action research, you are able to ensure the student is successful and receives the needed supports in all settings and classrooms within the school. Your research has a broad impact for the student(s)!

RATIONALE FOR SHARING DATA WITH EDUCATION COMMUNITY

While it is important to share what you have learned with your colleagues, there is also a lot of validity to sharing your research with others in the education community. You may be required to share with your university classmates, but you should also consider disseminating your learning beyond that.

There was a time when researchers did not share what they learned with others. You may have heard of the famous scientist and mathematician Isaac Newton, but did you know that he was reported to have kept his scientific discoveries secret because he feared that others would claim them as their own work (National Academy of Sciences et al., 2009)? While the world did eventually learn about Newton's work, there was a stretch of time when nobody other than him knew about gravity or the basics of calculus. Keeping the information to himself did not help the scientific community! Don't be like Isaac Newton—share your research! When you share what you learn through your action research, you are increasing the research base, as well as the evidence-based support for the specific intervention and its use with certain populations of students (Piwowar et al., 2008). And, because of copyright laws and the peer review process, you don't need to share Isaac Newton's concern and worry about your work being stolen by another researcher.

In the field of special education, a significant portion of the research that creates the evidence-base for a specific intervention is through single-case research methods (Maggin et al., 2018). It is likely that your action research study was a single-case research method; when combined with the research of other special educators, the work you have done will help create the research basis that supports the use of the intervention you chose (or the research that shows that the intervention is ineffective).

SHARING YOUR RESEARCH WITH THE EDUCATION COMMUNITY THROUGH PRESENTATIONS

Now that we have established that you should share your research with others, we need to talk about how you can do this. One way that you can share your research is through a presentation. You might be asked to present to your classmates or colleagues. You might present at a conference. Or you might decide to participate in a three-minute thesis competition or do a webinar. All of these are great ways to share what you have learned with others and, in this section, I offer some tips for doing each of these types of presentations.

In many action research courses, your professor will ask you to share your research with your classmates. This might be through a live presentation or it might be an online presentation (possibly similar to a webinar). Whatever the format, be sure that you first look at the instructions, guidelines, and grading rubric provided by your professor. You want to ensure that you are meeting the expectations for the presentation! Next, think about your audience. For a class presentation, you will likely know the audience and have probably taken several classes with them. Their background knowledge about special education and action research may be similar to yours. That means that you won't need to spend much (if any) time in your presentation explaining the purpose of doing action research nor the basics of special education. You can just dig right into the good stuff and start talking about your project. You will want to start by explaining the problem statement—tell your classmates why you selected this specific student and why you chose to focus on the learning or behavior challenge. Then, share a quick review of the literature on the topic. However, remember that your classmates don't need an in-depth review of the research. Provide them with the big themes and ideas found in the literature. I also recommend offering a reference list at the end so that your classmates can go look at the research themselves if they are interested in doing so.

After discussing the research, explain the intervention and results. Use visuals to show your data. You may consider showing a data chart similar to figure 5.1. Finally, discuss what you learned and the implications in your own classroom. Because action research is focused on improving our own practice and enhancing outcomes for our own students, this is the most critical part of the presentation. Textbox 6.1 lists the steps I just discussed.

A second way that you can share your action research is through a presentation at either a local or national conference. Your university might have a student research symposium or there may be a local teacher conference that would be appropriate. In addition, several national and international organizations in special education welcome presentations from students on their own research. The biggest special education professional organization, the Council for Exceptional Children, offers a special session of student presentations, known as Kaleidoscope. This is a great way to practice presenting, get feedback from experienced researchers, and meet other students doing research in their own classrooms.

When you consider presenting at a conference, you can select to do a full presentation, or you can do a poster session. If you choose to do an oral presentation, you will want to structure it in a manner similar to a presentation you would give to classmates, but be sure that you include plenty of time for questions and discussion from the audience. Another way to present action research at a conference is through a poster session. These sessions are opportunities to showcase your work and have one-to-one conversations with conference attendees about your research. For student researchers, I highly recommend the poster sessions as these individual conversations with other educators can help

Using UDL to Engage Online Teacher Education Candidates

Maria J. Lohmann
Colorado Christian University

Framing the Study
- 11% of college students have a disability (National Center for Education Statistics, 2016)
- Online classrooms include nontraditional students
- Universal Design for Learning (UDL) can reduce barriers to learning (Doolittle Wilson, 2017)
- Engagement in learning impacts achievement (Wonglorsaichon et al., 2014)

Professor Implemented Engagement Techniques in Online Courses
- Calling each student
- Online office hours
- Availability via phone, text, email
- Weekly Twitter chats
- Weekly optional course meetings

Open-ended survey to better understand impact of engagement techniques
- 20 respondents (response rate of 65%)
- Reponses coded by theme:
  - Connection to classmates/peers
  - Connection to course content
  - Application of UDL in own classrooms
  - Drawbacks of UDL use

Further Research
- Building relationships in online classrooms
- Impact of UDL on student learning
- Impact of engagement strategies for hybrid courses
- Impact of UDL on teacher candidates' future classroom instruction

Lohmann, M. J., Boothe, K.A., Hathcote, A. R., & Turpin, A. (2018). Engaging graduate students in the online learning environment: A Universal Design for Learning (UDL) approach to teacher preparation. Networks: An Online Journal for Teacher Research, 20(2), Article 5.

FIGURE 6.1. Action Research Project Poster.

Adapted from Engaging graduate students in the online learning environment: A Universal Design for Learning (UDL) approach to teacher preparation, by M. J. Lohmann, K. A. Boothe, A. R. Hathcote, & A. Turpin, 2018, Networks: An Online Journal for Teacher Research, 20(2), Article 5. CC BY 4.0.

you learn to articulate your research and will offer you practical ideas for your future research. In addition, the individualized aspect of poster sessions allows you to build conversations with leaders in the field of special education. When designing your poster, you will want to ensure that it is visually appealing and provides a good overview of your action research. Figure 6.1 provides a sample poster that highlights an action research project a colleague and I conducted in our online courses.

As you look at the sample poster, you will notice that bullet points are used in lieu of full sentences and that only the highlights of the research are presented. This is intentional. Poster presentations are designed to capture the interest of stakeholders and lead to individual discussions about the research and its implication. In addition, when posters are too wordy or offer too much information, they can be hard for stakeholders to read and understand. Keep in mind that you will have the opportunity to share more information and discuss the details of your research through the one-to-one conversations with attendees, so your poster does not need to showcase all of the information.

Another opportunity to share your research is through the three-minute thesis project, also known as 3MT. This project challenges student researchers to present their research in three minutes and in a manner that can be understood by people outside their field of expertise. Some universities have official 3MT competitions, but you can also take the challenge on your own and post your video to YouTube or a similar online platform. If you choose to share your

TABLE 6.1. Videos of 3-minute thesis

Rob Duguid, 2017 winner at Miami University	https://www.youtube.com/watch?v=dexCh39jEg4
Megan Pozzi, 2013 winner of QUT competition	https://www.youtube.com/watch?v=0K9iYUBCG_o
Matthew Thompson, 2011 winner at University of Western Australia	https://www.youtube.com/watch?v=pvjPzsLlyGw
Samuel Ramsey, 2017 winner at University of Maryland	https://www.youtube.com/watch?v=Fyfyj-2O47Q
Nusaiba Baker, 2018 winner at Georgia Tech	https://www.youtube.com/watch?v=ZFXiLXmdvrA
Mariam Elmarsafy, 2019 winner at Wilfrid Laurier University	https://www.youtube.com/watch?v=TVDt4zkduw0

research through a three-minute thesis, you need to ensure that your presentation tells a story that engages the audience, clearly explains your study and what you learned, and provides information that will support other teachers in using your research findings in their own classrooms. Table 6.1 offers examples of three-minute thesis presentations that you can view.

As you view the videos from table 6.1, you will notice that the presenters are excited about their topic. They each used body movements and facial expressions to show their passion for the topic. In addition, all of the presenters explained the research they conducted and gave the audience a concluding remark that either summarized the main point of the research or challenged audience members to act on the results. You will also notice that some speakers choose to use visual supports, such as pictures of PowerPoint presentations, while others did not. As you think about doing a three-minute thesis, you will first need to write a script. Textbox 6.2 provides a script for a 3MT that a researcher could present about the same research presented via poster in figure 6.1.

In addition to class presentations, conference presentations, or a three-minute thesis, you might also have the opportunity to present your research by hosting a webinar for teachers or talking to the other teachers at your school during a faculty meeting. When you are offered the chance to share your research, I urge you to take that opportunity. Remember that sharing your research benefits children beyond your own classroom! When presenting to colleagues, be sure to provide a quick overview of the action research process (you can use the visual you created in the chapter 1 questions to guide you) and explain why this process is important in the special education classroom. You will also need to offer a brief explanation of the previous research, but don't dwell on this. Focus most of your presentation on your action research project and its implications for the student and other students in your school or district. As you prepare to present to colleagues, I want to remind you, though, that when you present to

TEXTBOX 6.2
SAMPLE 3MT SCRIPT

Have you ever taken an online class or attended a remote training? After the past few years, I suspect we have all spent more time that we wanted on Zoom or Google Meets! Some of our online experiences have been good and some have left a bad taste in our mouths. Well, even before COVID-19 changed our lives, I was teaching future special education teachers in fully asynchronous online courses. That meant that they had their coursework available for them to complete on their own whenever and wherever they chose, as long as they met all assignment due dates.

My role as an online professor involves the facilitation of learning, but not always in real time. I quickly realized that this format did not offer me the chance to connect with my students. As an educator, I know that students who feel engaged and connected with their professors, classmates, and the learning content are more likely to be academically successful. With this in mind, a colleague and I designed an action research project to see if I could enhance student learning through building connections.

I selected a handful of previously researched techniques that showed an increase in student engagement and were reasonable for me to incorporate into my high teaching load. First, I called each student during the first week of class. In these phone calls, I introduced myself, welcomed students to the class, and encouraged them to reach out to me if they needed any support during the course. Second, I hosted weekly online office hours so that students could meet with me to get questions answered in real time. I also offered multiple ways for students to contact me, including email, text messages, and phone calls, and made myself available to be contacted during nontraditional hours that aligned with student free times. In addition, I hosted weekly Twitter chats for students in all my classes to connect with one another and discuss a topic of interest. Finally, for each class I taught that semester, I hosted a weekly live class session so that students could meet one another and discuss the course content together. Each of these activities was optional for students, and most students chose not to participate in them. At the end of the semester, my colleague and I sent a survey to the students in my courses and received a 65% response rate. The results of the survey indicated that, even if they never participated in the optional activities, the students appreciated the numerous ways to connect with me, one another, and the content. In addition, they noted that my efforts to engage them in learning helped them better understand how to engage and motivate students in their own classrooms.

Based on this action research, as well as additional studies, my colleague and I have concluded that online instructors can enhance the student experience through the use of intentional strategies to engage the learners. The next time that you are in an online meeting, I urge you to think about how you can increase the motivation and engagement of your colleagues!

TEXTBOX 6.3
PRESENTATION ACCESSIBILITY TIPS

- Use strong contrast between slide color and text color (e.g., black text on white background)
- Orally describe images used on slides
- Use sans serif fonts of 18-point or higher
- Ensure slides have plenty of white space
- Use visual images only as appropriate
- Closed caption or transcribe recorded presentations

---

stakeholders, you need to ensure that you are protecting student confidentiality. Do not use the real name of the student in your presentation; either choose a pseudonym or refer to them as "my student." While it is likely that many of the teachers in your school will know what student you are describing, it is vital that you do your best to ensure confidentiality. Personal information, such as the student's name, should only be shared with the stakeholders who need to know, such as the members of the student's IEP team.

As you consider doing a presentation, I also want to remind you that your presentation must be accessible for persons with disabilities. You don't want your presentation method to be a barrier to someone accessing what you have learned! As special educators, accessibility should always in our minds and should be a consideration in everything we do. Textbox 6.3 provides a few quick tips for ensuring that your action research presentation is accessible.

SHARING YOUR RESEARCH WITH THE EDUCATION COMMUNITY THROUGH AN ACTION RESEARCH JOURNAL ARTICLE

In addition to sharing what you learned in presentations, you can also share your action research by writing and publishing in peer-reviewed journals. There are several journals that focus on publishing action research conducted by teachers. Each of the journals has a different format and unique expectations, so you will want to ensure that you spend time reading articles published in that journal before you begin writing your own manuscript. A few of these journals are presented in table 6.2.

After you look at these journals, you will likely notice that the focus is on the discussion and implications of the research. Action research journals want authors to consider their own learning and how the research will continue to inform their own teaching. In addition, articles that are published in these journals present recommendations for other teachers and professionals working with students in the classroom.

TABLE 6.2. Action research journals for teachers

Journal name	Website
The Journal of Teacher Action Research	http://www.practicalteacherresearch.com/
Networks: An Online Journal for Teacher Research	https://newprairiepress.org/networks/
Educational Action Research	https://www.tandfonline.com/toc/reac20/current
Inquiry in Education	https://digitalcommons.nl.edu/ie/
The Canadian Journal of Action Research	https://journals.nipissingu.ca/index.php/cjar

SHARING YOUR RESEARCH WITH THE EDUCATION COMMUNITY THROUGH A JOURNAL ARTICLE

In addition to journals that focus solely on action research, your project may be appropriate for publication in a traditional special education journal. In order to determine the most appropriate outlet for publishing your work, you should consider the scope of your research (how many students, the length of time it was conducted, etc.), the generalizability of your action research, and your own preparedness to write a traditional research article. Keep in mind that because action research journals focus more on reflection and the impact that the research will have on your classroom, they may be easier for you to write, especially if you have not previously written a journal article. Do not, however, let the fact that you may be new to writing research articles discourage you from writing an article for a traditional journal.

If you determine that a traditional research journal is the best outlet for sharing your research with the broader community, you need to be aware of how to write these articles. I am going to share the basics with you below, but I highly recommend talking to your professor and reading published articles to better understand what is required. A traditional research journal article will include the following components: (a) introduction, (b) methodology, (c) results, and (d) discussion. The introduction section will introduce the research study and provide a brief review of the previous research on the topic. In the methodology section, you will share the research design—think back to the IRB form that you completed. The research design is that step-by-step process for implementing the intervention you outlined, as well as an explanation of how you analyzed the data. The results section is where you present your data—what was the result of implementing your intervention? The final portion of your article, the discussion section, is where you will share what your research means for the broader education community. In this section, you will (a) summarize your study in just a few sentences, (b) share how your research can support other teachers in meeting the needs of students with disabilities, (c) connect your research findings to previous research, which you likely presented in the introduction, (d) explain the limitations to your research (for action research, the limited sample size is almost always one of these limitations), and (e) offer suggestions of future research that should be conducted to help the field of special education better understand how to support students with a special learning or behavior challenge.

In my experience, students often find the introduction section the be the most challenging aspect to write. When you think about writing an introduction, I suggest looking at a dozen or so research articles and focusing on the first few pages—this is the introduction. The introduction is the literature review section of your journal article. This is not to be confused with a journal article that is completely a review of the literature. The literature review portion of a journal article is a discussion of the previous research that has been conducted on the topic. While this part of your journal article will likely only be a few pages in length, it should offer a solid overview of the existing research on the topic and should reference at last a handful of peer-reviewed research studies written by a variety of authors. For a topic that has been widely researched, you should include more references. In this part of the article, you will look for themes among the research. Consider the following questions:

1. What did all (or most) of the researchers you read find about the topic? What were the big themes? To find this answer, pay close attention to the results and discussion sections of the articles.
2. What were the differences between studies. For example, did researchers note that the intervention was more effective for elementary students than for high school students? Or, do the studies that used the intervention for children with autism find it to be effective while those who used the intervention for children with learning disabilities report that the intervention was ineffective?
3. What gaps in the research exist? Look closely at the discussion section of the articles, especially where they present the limitations. In addition, think about the specific populations that were studied. If your action research fills any gaps that exist, be sure to mention this in your introduction.
4. What data is relevant to the information you will present? For example, I frequently conduct research related to online learning in universities. It is important for readers to know the percentage of college students that take online courses, as well as what the nation-wide data says about the demographics of these students. With this in mind, I always share this data from government reports at the beginning of articles.

I hope that this provides you a bit more understanding of the introduction portion of a traditional journal article. To help you conceptualize this even more, textbox 6.4 provides a sample introduction. Please keep in mind that this sample is not published anywhere other than here. In fact, this is part of a project I did on teenage runaways when I was a graduate student. I specifically chose to share this example with you so that you can see what an introduction written by a graduate student might look like. Your first attempt at writing a journal article will likely not be perfect, and that is OK. Do not compare yourself to experienced researchers.

As you read the literature review, notice that I have focused on presenting themes that I found in the literature. In addition, you can see that the introduction concludes with a transition into the fictional study, which looks at the impact of mental health services in the school setting for teenage students who have previously run away from home.

TEXTBOX 6.4
SAMPLE LITERATURE REVIEW

Limited research is available regarding youth who run away from their homes in the United States and this lack of research may be a problem worldwide (Tam et al., 2008). According to the Office of Applied Studies, Substance Abuse, and Mental Health Services (2004), over one and a half million American youth ran away from home in 2002. There are some common characteristics that are shared by many adolescent runaways and can be used to determine a youth's chances of becoming a runaway. Common characteristics include age (Martinez, 2006; Thompson & Pillai, 2006; Tyler et al., 2001), gender (Martinez, 2006; Office of Applied Studies, Substance Abuse, and Mental Health Services, 2004), ethnicity (Thompson & Pillai, 2006; Tyler et al., 2001), living situation (Thomspon & Pillai, 2006), mental health problems (Martinez, 2006; Thompson & Pollio, 2006), having been sexually abused (Chen et al., 2004), and having a history of drug and alcohol use and/or abuse (Chen et al., 2004; Office of Applied Studies, Substance Abuse, and Mental Health Services, 2004; Thompson & Pillai, 2006).

The literature has identified common reasons that American teenagers run away from home, including: (a) family conflicts (Martinez, 2006), (b) neglect (Thompson & Pillai, 2006), (c) substance use or abuse by a parent (Martinez, 2006), and (d) abuse and violence by family members (Martinez, 2006; Thompson & Pollio, 2006). Other less common reasons that youth run away include the following: (a) legal problems, (b) problems in school, (c) running away to be with a friend, and (d) running to get away from various problems in their personal lives (Martinez, 2006).

Running away from home leads to short-term, as well as long-term, outcomes for juveniles. Some of these behaviors include (a) the use of drugs (Martinez, 2006; Office of Applied Studies, Substance Abuse, and Mental Health Services, 2004), (b) sexual activity (Fisher et al., 2001; Tyler et al., 2001), (c) involvement in a gang (Martinez, 2006), and (d) involvement in the selling of drugs (Martinez, 2006).

Runaway episodes can last for varying lengths of time and end for a variety of reasons. Martinez (2006) has identified several causes that lead to a runaway adolescent returning home. These include (a) missing their family members, (b) missing their homes, (c) being pregnant, (d) having a child at home, (e) becoming tired of living on the streets and hiding from the people that are looking for them, and (f) feeling that the streets are too dangerous. In addition, some youth return home because there is a lack of resources to meet their needs on the street (Tyler et al., 2001). Recidivism is a common problem among runaway teenagers (Martinez, 2006; Thompson & Pollio, 2006; Tyler et al., 2001).

Over 80% of homeless teenagers, including those who have run away from home, have a psychiatric disorder (Family and Youth Services Bureau, 2022). Communities need to address the mental health needs of youth, both before they run away and after they are already on the streets by providing services and adult assistance to the youth who need it (Baker et al., 2003; Martinez, 2006). Because children are legally mandated to attend school until at least the age of sixteen (National Center for Education Statistics, 2017), schools are uniquely positioned to support these mental health needs. Previous research has found that school-based mental health counseling is one method for meeting the mental health needs of high school students (Calderella et al., 2019; Das et al., 2016; Werner-Seidler et al., 2017). This study presents the results of a project designed to evaluate the impact of intensive mental health counseling provided in the school setting and the number of students in the community who run away from home.

References

Baker, A. J. L., McKay, M. M., Lynn, C. J., Schlange, H., & Auville, A. (2003). Recidivism at a shelter for adolescents: First-time versus repeat runaways. *Social Work Research, 27,* 84–93.

Calderella, P., Millet, A. J., Heath, M. A., Warren, J. S., & Williams, L. (2019). School counselors use of social emotional learning in high school: A study of the Strong Teens Curriculum. *Journal of School Counseling, 17*(19). http:/www.jsc.montana.edu/articles/v17n19.pdf

Chen, X., Tyler, K.A., Whitbeck, L.B., & Hoyt, D.R. (2004). Early sexual abuse, street adversity, and drug use among female homeless and runaway adolescents in the Midwest. *Journal of Drug Issues, 34,* 1–21.

Das, J. K., Salam, R. A., Lassi, Z. S., Khan, M. N., Mahmood, W., Patel, V., & Bhutta, Z. A. (2016). Interventions for adolescent mental health: An overview of systematic reviews. *Journal of Adolescent Health, 59*(4), S49–S60. https://doi.org/10.1016/j.jadohealth.2016.06.020

Family and Youth Services Bureau. (2022). Runaway and homeless youth, mental health, and trauma-informed care. https://rhyclearinghouse.acf.hhs.gov/blog/2019/03/runaway-and-homeless-youth-mental-health-and-trauma-informed-care

Fisher, D. G., Wilson, P. J., & Queen, M. S. (2001). Sexual and drug-taking experiences reported by runaway youth. *Journal of Alcohol and Drug Education, 40,* 88–99.

Martinez, R. J. (2006). Understanding Runaway Teens. *Journal of Child and Adolescent Psychiatric Nursing, 19,* 77–88.

National Center for Education Statistics. (2017). *Compulsory school attendance laws.* https://nces.ed.gov/programs/statereform/tab5_1.asp

Office of Applied Studies, Substance Abuse, and Mental Health Services Administration. (2004). *The NSDUH report: National survey on drug use and health.* Author.

Tam, K.Y., Zhao, M., Bullock, L.M., Lin, F., Chen, P., & Lin, S. (2008). *Along the train track: Runaway children and youth in China.*

Tyler, K.A., Hoyt, D.R., Whitbeck, L.B., & Cauce, A.M. (2001). The impact of childhood sexual abuse on later sexual victimization among runaway youth. *Journal of Research on Adolescence, 11,* 151–76.

Werner-Seidler, A., Perry, Y., Calear, A. L., Newby, J. M., & Christensen, H. (2017). School-based depression and anxiety prevention programs for young people: A systematic review and meta-analysis. *Clinical Psychology Review, 51*(1), 30–47. https://doi.org/10.1016/j.cpr.2016.10.005

CONCLUSION

It is vital that we collaborate with other educators by sharing what we learn in our own classrooms, including the results of our action research. When we share our findings, we as a field can make better decisions and better support the needs of students with disabilities. This chapter provided you with the tools to disseminate your action research. You can present your findings through a class presentation, at a conference, or by doing a 3TM. Or you can write an article in either an action research journal or a traditional journal based on your research. However, you choose to share your research is great, just be sure to share it!

REVIEW QUESTIONS AND EXERCISES

1. I have heard the saying that knowledge is a form of currency. Consider this statement and reflect on what it means to treat knowledge like money. Create a visual representation, such as a Venn diagram, that shows similarities and differences between knowledge and money as it applies to the school setting.

2. Consider the example of Isaac Newton provided in this chapter. Create an infographic showing the importance of sharing research and the potential downsides to not doing so. Help others understand why they should not be like Isaac Newton.

3. As you conclude your own action research, you need to make a plan for how you will share what you have learned. Choose one of the options listed in this chapter and prepare to share your research. Develop a step-by-step plan for doing so and share this plan with your classmates.

4. The final portion of this chapter provides a sample journal article introduction. Write a one-to-two-page literature review that you can use to introduce your action research to stakeholders. Be sure to focus on presenting the themes that you found in the previous research. In addition, ensure that you connect your action research to the previous research that has been conducted.

Conclusion

....

Student Learning Objectives

After reading chapter 7 and completing the exercises at the end of the chapter, students will be able to do the following:

- Describe the steps of the special education action research process
- Plan for and implement an action research project
- Share what they have learned about action research with stakeholders
- Articulate the role of action research in the IEP process

You have now reached the final chapter of this book. Over the past six chapters, you have learned the basic concepts of action research and how this process can support instruction in your classroom. As discussed in chapter 1, the action research process is simply the scientific method adjusted to meet the needs of teachers and students. The scientific method has six steps:

1. Observing a problem or phenomena that the researcher would like to better understand
2. Collecting initial (or baseline) data about the problem
3. Considering potential explanations for the situation and form a hypothesis
4. Designing an experiment, or series of experiments, to test that hypothesis
5. Carrying out the experiment and analyzing the results
6. Sharing the new knowledge or form a new hypothesis if the experiment results did not support the hypothesis (Voit, 2019)

These same steps to research apply regardless of the setting in which you are conducting research. When conducting action research in the special education classroom, we use each of these steps as outlined in figure 7.1. Each of the steps is critical. You cannot skip a step.

....

Identify a problem

⇓

Collect baseline data

⇓

Research evidence-based intervention

⇓

Select and implement an appropriate intervention

⇓

Collect data to determine the effectiveness of the intervention

⇓

Make adjustments to intervention plan to meet student needs

FIGURE 7.1. Flowchart of Special Education Action Research Process

A SYNOPSIS OF THE ACTION RESEARCH PROCESS

As a reminder, these action research steps work together to aid you in support-ing student learning and behavior in your classroom and school. The first step is to identify the problem. Remember that this could be a learning or behav-ior challenge of any intensity level. The challenge might be specific to one stu-dent, a group of students, or an entire classroom or school. Second, you will collect baseline data to help you gain a better understanding of the learning or behavior challenge. You will use this data to write a problem statement that identifies the challenge in observable and measurable terms and describes how the student's learning is impacted by the challenge. Third, you will look at the current research on the student challenge (or similar challenges), as well as the research on interventions that might support the student. After looking at the research, you will select an evidence-based intervention to implement with fidelity. During implementation, you will collect ongoing formative data that will aid you in identifying the effectiveness of the intervention. Based on the data you collect over several weeks, you will adjust or change the intervention as necessary. Throughout the entire process, you will take ongoing data, collab-orate with other stakeholders, and keep the unique needs of the student(s) as your focus.

ACTION RESEARCH AND THE INDIVIDUALIZED EDUCATION PROGRAM

As special education teachers, our jobs are strongly guided by the legal requirements as outlined in the Individuals with Disabilities Education Act of 2004 (IDEA, 2004). As mentioned in chapter 1 of this book, this law mandates the use of evidence-based practices for supporting our students. The use of EBPs is also legally mandated under the Every Student Succeeds Act (ESSA). You can find the exact verbiage from these laws in table 1.1. Action research helps us identify appropriate interventions and teaching methods. But this process also plays other vital roles in the Individualized Education Program (IEP) process.

Through the use of action research, we discover the teaching strategies, accommodations, and assistive technologies that benefit our students. As discussed in chapter 6, we share this information with other stakeholders, including all of the IEP team members. Then, we as a team, use the information to help us develop an appropriate IEP for our students.

The exact impact of the action research on IEP decision-making will depend upon the intervention you selected and the results you found. In many cases, the intervention used may demonstrate the need for an accommodation or assistive technology that supports a student's needs. When this happens, we must ensure that we include that tool or support in the student's IEP document. It is vital that we always include this information in the IEP so that future teachers and related service providers know what the student needs to be successful and so that we have written documentation of the support that is being provided to the student. Table 7.1 offers examples of action research projects that may lead to information about accommodations or assistive technologies.

Some action research projects investigate tools to support the challenging behaviors of students with disabilities. In these cases, the data you collect and the information you learn should be used to guide the Functional Behavioral Assessment (FBA) and behavior intervention plan (BIP) process. When we conduct an FBA, we gather data from a variety of sources to better understand the behavior challenge and then use that data to design an individualized BIP that specifically targets the challenging behavior and its function (Moreno & Bullock, 2011). This FBA and BIP process is precisely what we have talked about in this book. Remember that we discussed collecting baseline data in chapter 2 and then used that data to select an intervention that may support our student's needs, tested out that intervention, evaluated the effectiveness, and made adjustments as necessary. This action research process is the same process that you follow when conducting an FBA and writing a BIP. Knowing that these two processes are very similar, you should document your action research on behavior challenges within your school district FBA/BIP forms. But remember that this is a team process, so you will need to be diligent about sharing your

TABLE 7.1. Action research and accommodations and assistive technologies

Action research scenario	Impact on IEP Document
George's teacher conducted an action research project in which she created a visual schedule to help reduce his frustration during transitions. George's challenging behaviors decreased once he learned to use the visual schedule.	"Visual schedule" should be added to the assistive technology and accommodations sections of George's individualized education program (IEP).
Amari does not meet grade-level expectations for reading comprehension, so her teacher conducted an action research project to understand the impact of pairing reading with listening to a book read aloud. While Amari is not yet at grade level, her reading comprehension is consistently improving.	"Audiobook or book read aloud" should be added as an accommodation in Amari's IEP.
Dante is a fourth-grade student and has been struggling with mathematics. In previous years, he was one of the best students in this subject, so his teacher investigated what has changed. She discovered that mathematics tests in her classroom are always in the afternoons, while Dante's previous teachers gave tests in the morning. The teacher conducted an action research project to determine if the time of day that testing was occurring impacted Dante's success. She learned that Dante's mathematics scores were significantly higher when the tests were given in the morning.	"Exams and tests given in the morning" should be included as an accommodation in Dante's IEP.
Calliope is a nonverbal kindergarten student with autism. In order to support Calliope's communication needs, her teacher and speech-language pathologist worked together to conduct an action research project that investigated the impact Calliope's language when using a simple augmentative and alternative communication (AAC) device. Calliope is now communicating with peers and adults several times each day using her device.	"AAC device" should be included in the assistive technology section of Calliope's IEP.

data with other IEP team members and soliciting their advice in selecting and evaluating interventions.

Finally, your action research project may help you better understand a student's learning progress. This information can assist you as a write IEP goals. For example, consider the scenario of Julian below.

Mr. Franklin and his paraprofessionals have implemented an appropriate reading intervention for Julian, and eight weeks of data shows a trend that his reading fluency is increasing by one word per minute. When the IEP team meets for Julian's annual review meeting, they look at the reading intervention data. Based on the progress that Julian is making, they decide to write a reading fluency IEP goal and use the current data to determine an appropriate goal. There are 36 weeks of school, not counting the extended school year (ESY), in the school district. The team knows that Julian may miss a few days of school due to being sick but will also be attending ESY over the summer. So, the team decides to write Julian's fluency goal to indicate a fluency increase of 36 words per minute. Currently, Julian is reading 48 words per minute on a second-grade DIBELS reading passage. The IEP team writes the following goal into Julian's IEP: "By the next IEP annual review meeting, Julian will independently read 84 words per minute on a second-grade DIBELS reading fluency assessment."

As you can see, the use of action research can and should be used to guide IEP decision making. Action research provides special educators with valuable data and information that supports individual student learning. As you think about the action research you have conducted, consider how you will use what you have learned to support writing your students' IEPs.

CONSIDERATIONS FOR DATA IN SPECIAL EDUCATION

While all teachers should be collecting data and using that data to drive their instruction, the use of data-based decision making is even more critical in the special education classroom. Your work is almost entirely driven by the data you collect. You use the data to determine whether a student needs special education services in order to be successful, to assess the effectiveness of a specific intervention for meeting a student's need, to evaluate student progress, and as a means of communicating success to stakeholders. As this book concludes, I want to remind you of a few critical considerations regarding the use of data for decision making in the special education classroom.

First, be sure that you keep the data you collect confidential. Student educational records, including school-based data, are protected by the Family Educational Rights and Privacy Act (FERPA). Per the requirements of this law, data can be shared with educational stakeholders, such as school employees. With this in mind, though, it should only be disclosed as appropriate to relevant stakeholders, which may include (a) the student, (b) the students' family, (c) other teachers or school administrators, and (d) related service providers. If others, such as paraprofessionals, are helping you to collect data, you must ensure that they understand the requirements for ensuring confidentiality. Teachers commonly collect data using paper-based forms or apps on their phones. When doing this, be sure that students cannot see the data you are collecting about their classmates.

Second, your action research and the data you collect must be individualized to the specific needs of the student(s) and the classroom. Because each student and classroom is unique, their needs will differ from those of other students. Be sure that you keep this in mind when selecting interventions for a specific student. An intervention being effective for one student is not a guarantee of effectiveness for other students. Use your data to determine what is working and make changes as needed.

Third, some colleagues and IEP members may have less experience with action research and data collection than you do. Be prepared to share your data in an easy-to-understand manner and to answer questions. In chapter 6, I offered examples of ways that you can share your data. I challenge you to identify ways that you can make the action research data you have collected relevant and meaningful for your student, their families, and the other teachers who also teach the student.

Finally, data is your friend as a special education teacher. The use of data is a critical part of your job and provides justification and a rationale for the work you are doing. This data is used in IEP meetings and also for conversations with stakeholders. Be diligent about collecting, analyzing, and organizing data. You are likely to be asked to share data with IEP team members or your school administrator and need to be ready to do so with little preparation. Be prepared to share your data.

MOVING FORWARD

Now that you have finished learning about action research, it is time to put your learning into practice in your own classrooms and schools. If you have not already done so, I challenge you to locate a learning or behavior challenge in your classroom and use the action research process to support your student(s). Remember that this process will take time, but it will be worth it.

Keep in mind that action research is different from traditional research in many ways. In this book, you have learned to use data to implement interventions to support student success in your own classroom and school. The research you are conducting will have immediate positive impacts on your own environment and will may help others. But the focus is on your classroom and your students. Good luck as you continue supporting all learners through data-based decision-making.

REVIEW QUESTIONS AND EXERCISES

1. Teachers must be lifelong learners and action research is one way that teachers can continue growing in their knowledge and skills to support all learners. In a short paragraph, explain the role of action research in teachers' professional development and discuss the potential impact on student learning when teachers do not continue to grow in their knowledge of teaching.

2. Think about the action research project that you conducted. Using the IEP form of your choice, write 1–2 SMART goals and complete the accommodations/modifications section of the IEP. Be sure to use what you learned in your action research to guide you.

3. Think about Billy from the vignettes at the beginning of each chapter. Based on what you read about this scenario, what information should Mr. Bullock include in Billy's IEP? Write one goal that you would put in his IEP and at least three accommodations or modifications that you would recommend including. Discuss your answer with a classmate.

4. As you finish reading this book, think about what you have learned. Create a 3–5-minute presentation that you can use to teach others about the special education action research process.

5. Consider how your understanding of action research and the use of data-based decision making in special education has changed as a result of reading this book. In addition, think about what you still want to know about the topic. Create a K-W-L (What I knew before reading this book, What I still want to know, What I learned from reading this book) chart about your understanding of the action research process.

Appendix A

Case Studies: Sample Action Research Projects

CASE STUDY: PIERRE

Overview

Pierre is an eleventh-grade student who has been diagnosed as having a specific learning disability. Mrs. Hathcote is his special education case manager and is also the teacher for his special education algebra class. As Pierre has completed math assignments this school year, Mrs. Hathcote has noticed that Pierre has not mastered his multiplication and division facts. She has noticed that Pierre often uses a calculator to find the answer to simple math facts before he can begin working on the more challenging components of the mathematical problem. Taking time to do this makes it challenging for Pierre to complete his math assignments in a timely manner, and the time it takes appears to make him frustrated many days. Mrs. Hathcote believes that Pierre would be more successful on his assignments and have a more positive attitude about mathematics if she can help him to become more fluent in his multiplication and division facts.

Problem Statement

Pierre has not mastered his multiplication and division facts. Not knowing these facts makes it challenging for Pierre to complete grade-level mathematics assignments. I want to conduct this action research to help Pierre become fluent in multiplication and division.

Evidence-Based Practices

Mrs. Hathcote has reviewed the literature on math fact fluency and has identified a variety of potential EBPs that may benefit Pierre. Specifically, she has read the research supporting the use of the following:

- Computer-assisted instruction (Hawkins et al., 2016)
- Taped problems intervention (McCallum & Schmitt, 2011)
- Cover, copy, and compare (Becker et al., 2009)
- Virtual manipulatives (Kabel et al., 2021)

After looking at the EBPs, Mrs. Hathcote designed an intervention plan using the taped problems intervention method.

Intervention Design

1. Mrs. Hathcote will record herself saying the ones, twos, threes, and fours times tables on the classroom iPad. Before saying the answer to each mathematical problem, she will pause for two seconds. For example, she will say, "One times one equals" and then wait two seconds before saying the answer, "One."
2. For the first five minutes of mathematics class each day, Pierre will independently listen to the audio recordings and answer the multiplication questions. He will be challenged to answer each problem before he hears Mrs. Hathcote provide the answer. While Pierre is doing this work, the rest of the class will be checking their homework from the previous night.
3. Each Friday, Pierre will complete a one-minute multiplication fluency probe. His math fact fluency will be compared to previous weeks.
4. After three weeks of intervention, the team will evaluate progress and adjust the intervention plan as needed

Intervention Data

Baseline: 10 facts per minute
Week 1: 15 facts per minute
Week 2: 18 facts per minute
Week 3: 25 facts per minute

Next Steps

Three weeks of data indicates that the intervention is effective for increasing Pierre's multiplication fact fluency. Based on this data, Mrs. Hathcote will continue using this intervention for Pierre. In Week 4, she will add the fives, sixes, and sevens multiplication facts. She will add the eights, nines, and tens in

Week 6. Starting in Week 8, Mrs. Hathcote will add division facts to the audio recording. Pierre will continue to be assessed using a facts fluency probe every Friday and the team will discuss the data at least once every three weeks.

Sharing the Research

Mrs. Hathcote knows that it is important to share what she is learning. She has graphed the data she collected and sent it to the rest of the IEP team. In addition, she called Pierre's parents to explain the data and get their feedback on the intervention. Finally, she has created a three-minute thesis presentation to share her action research with the other students in the university action research course she is currently taking.

CASE STUDY: JACK

Overview

Mrs. Wong provides both inclusion support and pull-out services for students in the first through third grades at Central Elementary School. Jack is a student on her caseload who is behind grade-level for reading fluency and comprehension. Mrs. Wong has provided small group instruction for Jack and the other third grade students who have reading disabilities, but Jack is not making progress.

Problem Statement

Jack is not meeting grade-level expectations for reading fluency and comprehension. Literacy skills impact success in all subject areas. If Jack is not able to read the content in all subjects, he will not be successful throughout the school day. I want to conduct this action research to support Jack's reading fluency and comprehension skills so that he can be successful. Over time, I want to use interventions that support fluency and interventions that support comprehension, but for this action research project, I will target fluency-based reading interventions.

Evidence-Based Practices

Mrs. Wong sees that there are numerous EBPs that support reading instruction and has identified three in particular that she believes might be appropriate for helping Jack.

- Systematic phonics instruction (Ehri, 2020)
- Technology-based small group tutoring (Madden & Slavin, 2017)
- Listening to passage read aloud paired with repeated readings (Lee & Yoon, 2017)

The school district recently supported Mrs. Wong in attending a Wilson Reading training. This intervention focuses on systematic phonics instruction. Because she has the training needed to implement the intervention, Mrs. Wong has decided to use the EBP of systematic phonics instruction in order to support Jack.

Intervention Design

1. Mrs. Wong will submit an application to her university IRB in order to get her research approved.

2. Mrs. Wong will review the materials she received during the Wilson Reading training.
3. Mrs. Wong learned in the training that Wilson can be implemented in either one-to-one settings or in small groups of up to six students. At this time, Jack and two other students are not making expected reading fluency progress, so Mrs. Wong will implement the Wilson program with the three students together.
4. Mrs. Wong will rearrange her daily intervention schedule to find a 30-minute block of time to provide the Wilson Reading System to the three students all five school days each week. Mrs. Wong knows that a 60–90-minute block of time is preferred, but she cannot dedicate this much time to the intervention while still meeting the needs of all learners on her caseload.
5. Mrs. Wong will follow the Wilson Reading System lesson plans and do one block of the lesson plan each day on Mondays, Wednesdays, and Fridays. This will allow her to complete one lesson each week. Tuesdays and Thursdays will be focused on review activities and progress monitoring.
6. Every Tuesday, Mrs. Wong will administer a third-grade DIBELS reading fluency probe.
7. Every two weeks, Mrs. Wong will take the DIBELS data, as well as classroom-based notes and work samples, to the special education team meeting to get additional perspectives on Jack's progress.

Intervention Data

Baseline: 50
Week 1: 51
Week 2: 51
Week 3: 54
Week 4: 60
Week 5: 65
Week 6: 68
Week 7: 70
Week 8: 71

Next Steps:

After reviewing eight weeks of intervention data, Mrs. Wong and the special education team determine that the Wilson Reading System is an effective intervention for increasing Jack's reading fluency and the intervention will be continued in its current format. Because Mrs. Wong wants to support both fluency and comprehension (and because the Wilson Reading System supports both of these areas), Mrs. Wong is going to start assessing Jack's reading comprehension through a cloze reading passage curriculum measurement every Thursday.

Sharing the Research:

Mrs. Wong wants to encourage other teachers to use the action research process to support student learning, so she decides to present her research in a poster presentation at her state Council for Exceptional Children (CEC) conference.

CASE STUDY: ALANA

Overview

Mr. Steere is a middle school resource teacher for an online school. This semester, there is one student, Alana, who frequently shows up to class late and often does not have the learning materials she needs when she logs into class. Alana will then leave remote learning while she gathers the materials she needs from her house. It is not uncommon for Alana to miss more than half of a class period as she is searching for the needed learning materials. Because Alana is learning from home, Mr. Steere is struggling to figure out how to support her.

Problem Statement

In order to learn grade-level content, children must be present in school. Alana is frequently late to class and, when she arrives, she often does not have the materials she needs. I want to conduct this action research to support Alana in being present and prepared for class so that she can be a successful student.

Evidence-Based Practices

Mr. Steere has extensive experience with supporting students who are unprepared for learning in the in-person school setting. He believes that some of the interventions that work for students in a traditional classroom may also work, with adaptations, in the remote classroom. After looking at the research and considering the resources he has available, he believes that three interventions may be appropriate.

1. Offering rewards/incentives for on-time attendance to class (Freeman et al., 2018)
2. Self-monitoring of arrival time (Bruhn et al., 2015)
3. Group contingency/class wide reward (Hulac & Benson, 2010)

In order to give Alana ownership over her own learning, Mr. Steere asks her to help him select the intervention to implement for the action research project. Alana states that getting a reward of reduced homework will incentivize her to arrive in the remote classroom online and with the needed materials.

Intervention Design

1. Mr. Steere creates a written contract that states the terms of the expectations, which include on-time arrival to class and having all required materials for the day.

2. Mr. Steere goes over the contract with both Alana and her parents. Mr. Steere, Alana, and her parents all sign the contract.

3. Mr. Steere creates a daily checklist that includes each of the expectations and each of the required materials for daily learning. The following items are included: (a) Alana arrived on time, (b) Alana had her homework ready to submit, (c) Alana had the textbook, (d) Alana had paper, (e) Alana had a writing utensil, (f) Alana had all other required learning materials as listed in the class Google Classroom calendar.

4. Each day, Mr. Steere and Alana will meet after class for two minutes to complete the checklist together.

5. On days when all boxes are checked on the checklist, Alana will select four questions that she does not need to complete on the daily assignment.

6. On days when Alana has not met all expectations, she will be expected to complete all questions on the daily assignment.

7. Every Friday, Mr. Steere and Alana will discuss her progress on the expectations.

8. Mr. Steere will email Alana's parents every Friday to provide an update

TABLE A.1. Intervention data

	On-Time	Homework	Textbook	Paper	Pencil	Other materials
Baseline	0/10 days	2/10 days	4/10 days	3/10 days	3/10 days	1/10 days
Week 1	4/5 days	4/5 days	4/5 days	4/5 days	4/5 days	4/5 days
Week 2	4/5 days	3/5 days	3/5 days	3/5 days	3/5 days	2/5 days
Week 3	0/5 days	2/5 days	2/5 days	1/5 days	1/5 days	0/5 days
Week 4	2/5 days	3/5 days	1/5 days	2/5 days	1/5 days	0/5 days
Week 5	1/5 days	3/5 days	2/5 days	2/5 days	2/5 days	0/5 days

Next Steps

After looking at the data, Mr. Steere concludes that the selected intervention is not working. While Alana started the first week of the intervention by mostly meeting expectations, she soon was no longer arriving to class on time and prepared. Mr. Steere knows that he needs to try a different intervention to help Alana be successful. He conducts additional research and collaborates with Alana's parents to design a new intervention. For the next several weeks, Alana's parents are going to call her five minutes before class every single day. During the phone call, they will make sure that she gathers the materials needed for class. They will stay on the phone with her until she logs into class. In addition, each evening, they will check to ensure she has completed her homework. Mr.

Steere will send them a daily email after class to confirm that Alana arrived at class on-time and prepared.

Sharing the Research

As he is conducting his action research, Mr. Steere is communicating with stakeholders, including Alana's parents and other teachers in the online school. As he reviewed the peer-reviewed research on increasing school attendance, Mr. Steere shared what he learned in a faculty meeting. He continues to share what he is learning about supporting Alana through weekly updates to her other teachers so that they can implement a similar intervention once he finds one that works for Alana.

Appendix B

....

Case Studies for Student Practice

Below, you will find ten case studies that you can use to practice the action research process. Please keep in mind that these case studies represent only a small number of the learning and behavior challenges you may encounter in your own classroom. They are not representative of all (or even most) student needs. For each case study, you will see the overview and baseline data. Based on that information, you will need to provide the following information. Your professor may ask you to select one case study or to complete them all.

1. A problem statement
2. A list of three to five evidence-based interventions that may be appropriate for supporting the student need. Be sure to include citations for research that support the use of each of these EBPs
3. A step-by-step intervention design
4. A plan for sharing your research
5. A list of other information that you want/need to know in order to best support the student. This may include additional baseline data you would like to collect, information about previous interventions that have been tried, specific information about the school/classroom/student/grade, or anything else you feel would be important in supporting the needs of the student.

CASE STUDY 1: COMMUNICATION DELAY IN PRESCHOOL

Overview

Mr. Phiri is an inclusive preschool teacher. His classroom includes students with disabilities, as well as typically developing preschoolers. Mary is in his class; she has been diagnosed with Down Syndrome. Due to her large tongue, Mary's speech can be hard to understand, especially for her classmates. Mr. Phiri has noticed that when her peers cannot understand Mary, they simply walk away and do not play with her. Mr. Phiri wants to find a way to help Mary communicate so that the other children can understand her as he knows that social interactions are critical for young children.

Baseline Data

Classmates walked away when Mary was talking in 19 out of 20 opportunities at recess over the course of one school week.

CASE STUDY 2: SELF-INJURY BEHAVIOR IN SIXTH GRADE

Overview

Mrs. Boothe is a middle school self-contained teacher for students with autism. One of her students, Gina, has recently begun banging her head against the wall when she gets frustrated. Because this behavior is dangerous, Mrs. Boothe wants to find a safe solution as soon as possible. She is looking for an alternative behavior for Gina that will allow her to express her frustration in a way that does not lead to harm.

Baseline Data

Over the course of three days, Gina banged her head against the wall ten times.

CASE STUDY 3: HYPERACTIVITY IN FIRST GRADE

Overview

Mr. Combes provides inclusion support for students with disabilities in the general education first-grade classroom. One of the students on his caseload, Bertina, has trouble focusing on the learning and frequently needs to be redirected to sit in her chair and look at the teacher. Bertina is struggling with the first-grade learning material and is behind her classmates in her reading skills and mathematical fact fluency. Mr. Combes would like to find a solution for helping Bertina stay focused as he believes this would help her be more successful in the classroom.

Baseline Data

Bertina required 24 redirections to pay attention during math lessons over the course of one week.

Bertina required 18 redirections to pay attention during language arts lessons over the course of one week.

CASE STUDY 4: PARAPROFESSIONAL TRAINING

Overview

Mrs. Lohmann is a self-contained teacher in a classroom for kindergarten through fifth-grade students who have been diagnosed with an emotional disturbance (ED). The students in her classroom spend most, if not all, of their day in Mrs. Lohmann's classroom, where they receive support from five paraprofessionals. Mrs. Lohmann has noticed that one of her paraprofessionals does not follow the protocol for behavior challenges as outlined in the students' BIPs. Instead, the paraprofessional often raises his voice at the students, which frequently seems to escalate the behavior.

Baseline Data

Paraprofessional raised his voice 12 times at Student A, 18 times at Student B, and 6 times at Student C over the course of 10 school days.

CASE STUDY 5: ELOPEMENT IN FOURTH GRADE

Overview

Ms. Khan teaches in a self-contained classroom for students with autism. Her classroom has two doors, one goes into the school hallway and the other goes outside into the school parking lot. Per city fire code regulations, Ms. Khan is required to leave both doors unlocked during school hours. Marvin is a fourth-grade student in Ms. Khan's classroom. He is nonverbal and communicates by pointing and grunting. Recently, Marvin has begun eloping from the classroom. "Elopement" is the term used to indicate that a student runs away from their classroom or other supervised area. The majority of times that he elopes, Marvin goes into the school hallway. However, he has exited the classroom through the door to outside a few times. Last week, he was able to run almost a mile before being caught. Ms. Khan wants to keep Marvin safe and is looking for a solution to stop the elopement behavior.

Baseline Data

Over the past two weeks, Marvin has eloped from the classroom an average of two times each day.

CASE STUDY 6: TRANSITION GOAL FOR HIGH SCHOOL STUDENT

Overview

Mr. Scott is the coordinator of a high school transition program and works with students between the ages of 18 and 21, with a focus on functional and life skills. Opal is a 20-year-old who receives special education services under the category of intellectual disabilities. Opal's transition plan includes the goal that she will learn to independently ride the bus to get from her home to her job at the bowling alley each day. In order to do this successfully, Opal must be able to identify the bus stops where she should get off near her home and her job and then signal to the bus driver to stop the bus at those stops. Mr. Scott, or a paraprofessional, have been riding with Opal on the bus every day this school year to help her practice learning to ride the bus. With their help, she is able to get off the bus at the appropriate stops. However, when they simply observe and do not assist her, Opal frequently misses her bus stop or does not indicate to the driver that they should stop the bus. Mr. Scott wants to ensure that Opal meets the goal in her transition plan.

Baseline Data

For the past month, Mr. Scott and his paraprofessional have observed Opal on the bus and not aided in helping her identify the bus stop. Out of 20 trials, Opal has successfully gotten off at the correct stop twice. Twelve times she did not notice that it was her stop, and six times she did not indicate to the driver to stop the bus.

CASE STUDY 7: CHEATING BEHAVIOR IN MIDDLE SCHOOL

Overview

Mrs. Habeck is a middle school special education teacher who provides direct supports to students in inclusive classrooms, as well as consultative supports to their teachers. During her weekly meeting with the general education teachers, both the language arts and social studies teachers expressed a concern that Destiny has been using her phone during class tests and quizzes. While they have been unable to prove it, they believe that she is cheating and has received the answers to the tests from a friend in an earlier class period. When asked to put the phone away, Destiny gets defensive, sighs, and puts the phone in her backpack. Mrs. Habeck knows that Destiny has been identified as having a learning disability and is below grade-level expectations in reading and writing, making both of these subjects challenging for her. She also knows that Destiny feels embarrassed by her learning needs. Mrs. Habeck wants to stop the cheating and help Destiny be successful in learning the course content for both language arts and social studies.

Baseline Data

This week, Destiny was caught using her phone during her spelling test in language arts, as well as three of the five daily social studies quizzes.

CASE STUDY 8: WRITING DISABILITY IN THIRD GRADE

Overview

Mr. Lopez is a special education teacher who co-teaches in a third-grade classroom. Hermione and Ophelia are students in the classroom and both have been identified as having a learning disability in the area of writing. Specifically, Mr. Lopez is concerned about their spelling and grammar when they write in their daily journals, as well as when they write short stories. Mr. Lopez wants to help both girls improve their writing skills and would like to find an intervention that he can use with both students together.

Baseline Data

Mr. Lopez gave the girls a writing prompt in order to collect baseline data. The prompt required the students to write one paragraph with five sentences. Hermione had a total of twelve spelling, three punctuation, and two capitalization errors in her paragraph. Ophelia had 22 spelling, 5 punctuation, and 6 capital-ization errors.

CASE STUDY 9: MATH DELAY IN SECOND GRADE

Overview

Matteo is a second-grade student who is currently being evaluated for special education services. Ms. Waterloo has noticed during both the formal assess-ments, as well as during observations, that Matteo takes longer than the other students in his class to complete the daily math facts worksheet and frequently mistakes the mathematical symbols. Ms. Waterloo wants to design an interven-tion to support Matteo in his mathematical skills

Baseline Data

Over the course of one week, Ms. Waterloo collected daily data from Matteo's math facts worksheet. Each worksheet included ten math problems, five addi-tion problems, and five subtraction problems. The data she collected is in the chart below.

TABLE B.1.   Matteo math intervention data

Day	Number correct	Time to complete worksheet	Comments
Monday	3/10	4 minutes, 15 seconds	Matteo answered all of the problems as addition problems.
Tuesday	5/10	2 minutes, 55 seconds	Matteo answered all of the problems as addition problems. He got each of the addition problems correct.
Wednesday	0/10	10 minutes	Matteo did not answer any math problems. After ten minutes, the classroom teacher took the worksheet.
Thursday	5/10	3 minutes, 30 seconds	Matteo answered all of the problems as addition problems. He got each of the addition problems correct.
Friday	5/10	2 minutes, 45 seconds	Matteo answered all of the problems as addition problems. He got each of the addition problems correct.

CASE STUDY 10: BITING BEHAVIOR IN KINDERGARTEN

Overview

Ms. Gupta supports children with disabilities in elementary school classrooms. Sammie is a kindergarten student who has been identified as having a developmental disability. Sammie has recently been biting the other students in his classroom. Ms. Gupta is unsure about the function of the biting behavior, but she wants to keep all of the students safe and help Sammie to interact appropriately with his classmates.

Baseline Data

Over the past four days, Sammie has bit a classmate nine times, with eight of those times occurring during Centers and the other time on the playground. Of the nine bites, four were on the same classmate. Five other classmates were each bitten one time.

References

···

Abualsaud, D. (2019). Men pause and women talk too much: Power and gender negotiations in eliciting data during semi-structured interviews. *Journal of Advanced Research in Social Sciences and Humanities, 4*(6), 210–23. https://dx.doi.org/10.26500/JARSSH-04-2019-0603

Alberto, P., & Troutman, A. C. (2012). *Applied behavior analysis for teachers* (9th ed.). Pearson.

Al-Riyami, A. (2008). How to prepare a research proposal. *Oman Medical Journal, 23*(2), 66–69.

Ary, D., Cheser Jacobs, L., Sorenson Irvine, C. K., & Walker, D. (2018). *Introduction to Research in Education* (10th ed). Cengage Learning.

Bailey, S. L., Pokrzywinski, J., & Bryant, L. E. (1983). Using water mist to reduce self-injurious and stereotypic behavior. *Applied Research in Mental Retardation, 4*(3), 229–241.

Barczak, M. A. (2019). Simulated and community-based instruction: Teaching students with intellectual and developmental disabilities to make financial transactions. *Teaching Exceptional Children, 51*(4), 313–21. https://doi.org/10.1177%2F0040059919826035

Beall, J. (2010). "Predatory" open-access scholarly publishers. *The Charleston Advisor, 11*(4), 10–17.

Beall, J. (2017). Predatory journals, peer review, and education research. *New Horizons in Adult Education & Human Resources Development, 29*(1), 54–58. https://doi.org/10.1002/nha3.20173

Beaver, J. M., & Carter, M. A. (2006). *The developmental reading assessment* (2nd ed.). Pearson.

Bittner, M., & Davis, M. T. (2019). Comparison of evidence-based practices for students with autism spectrum disorder. *Special Education: Research, Policy, & Practice, 3*(1), 88–106.

Boddy, C. R. (2016). Sample size for qualitative research. *Qualitative Market Research: An International Journal, 19*(4), 426–32. https://doi.org/10.1108/QMR-06-2016-0053

Borko, H., Roberts, S., & Shavelson, R. J. (2008). Teachers' decision making: From Alan J. Bishop to today. In P. Clarkson & N. Presmeg (Eds.) *Critical Issues in Mathematics Education* (pp. 37–67). Springer.

Bouck, E., Park, J., & Nickell, B. (2017). Using the concrete-representational-abstract approach to support students with intellectual disability to solve change-making problems. *Research in Developmental Disabilities, 60*, 24–36. https://doi.org/10.1016/j.ridd.2016.11.006

Brannen, J. (2017). *Mixing methods: Qualitative and quantitative research.* Taylor & Francis Group. https://doi.org/10.4324/9781315248813

Brawley, S., & Stormont, M. A. (2014). Investigating reported data practices in early childhood: An exploratory study. *Journal of Positive Behavior Interventions, 16*(2), 102–111. https://doi.org/10.1177%2F1098300713480838

···

Breitenstein, S. M., Gross, D., Garvey, C. A., Hill, C., Fogg, L., & Resnick, B. (2010). Implementation fidelity in community-based interventions. *Research in Nursing & Health, 33*(2), 164–73. https://doi.org/10.1002/nur.20373.

Brookhart, S. M. (2013). *How to create and use rubrics for formative assessment and grading.* ASCD.

Brookhart, S. M. (2018). Appropriate criteria: Key to effective rubrics. *Frontiers in Education, 3*(22). https://doi.org/10.3389/feduc.2018.00022

Brown, G. T., Lake, R., & Matters, G. (2011). Queensland teachers' conceptions of assessment: The impact of policy priorities on teacher attitudes. *Teaching and Teacher Education, 27*(1), 210–20. http://dx.doi.org/10.1016/j.tate.2010.08.003

Bruhn, A., McDaniel, S., & Kreigh, C. (2015). Self-monitoring interventions for students with behavior problems: A systematic review of current research. *Behavioral Disorders, 40*(2), 102–21. https://doi.org/10.17988%2FBD-13-45.1

Campbell, J. M., & Hammond, R. K. (2014). Best practices in rating scale assessment of children's behavior. In P. L. Harrison & A. Thomas (Eds.), *Best practices in school psychology: Data-based and collaborative decision making* (pp. 287–304). National Association of School Psychologists.

Carlson, D., Borman, G., & Robinson, M. (2011). A multistate district-level cluster randomized trial of the impact of data-driven reform on reading and mathematics achievement. *Educational Evaluation and Policy Analysis, 33*(3), 378–98. https://doi.org/10.3102%2F0162373711412765

Centers for Disease Control. (2014). *Establishing a baseline as part of your evaluation* [PowerPoint slides]. https://www.cdc.gov/dhdsp/pubs/docs/cb_jan2014.pdf

Cochran-Smith, M., & Lytle, S. L. (1993). *Inside and outside: Teacher research and knowledge.* Teachers College Press.

Colorado State University. (2021). *Creating Questionnaire Questions.* https://writing.colostate.edu/guides/pdfs/guide68.pdf

Common Core State Standards Initiative. (2021). *English Language Arts Standards.* http://www.corestandards.org/ELA-Literacy

Cook, B. G., Tankersley, M., Cook, L., & Landrum, T. J. (2008). Evidence-based practices in special education: Some practical considerations. *Intervention in School and Clinic, 44*(2), 69–75. https://doi.org/10.1177%2F1053451208321452

Cornelius, K. E. (2013). Formative assessment made easy: Templates for collecting daily data in inclusive classrooms. *Teaching Exceptional Children, 45*(5), 14–21. https://doi.org/10.1177%2F004005991304500502

Cox, E. (2019). *Characteristics of behavior rating scales: Revisited* (Paper No. 3103). Masters Theses & Specialist Projects. https://digitalcommons.wku.edu/theses/3103

Delucchi, M. (2014). Measuring student learning in social statistics: A pretest-posttest study of knowledge gain. *Teaching Sociology, 42*(3), 231–39. https://doi.org/10.1177%2F0092055X14527909

Deno, S. L., Fuchs, L. S., Marston, D., & Shin, J. (2001). Using curriculum-based measurements to establish growth standards for students with learning disabilities. *School Psychology Review, 30*(4), 507–24.

DiCarlo, C. F., Baumgartner, J. I., Caballero, J. L., & Powers, C. (2017). Using least-to-most assistive prompt hierarchy to increase child compliance with teacher directives in preschool classrooms. *Early Childhood Education Journal, 45*, 745–54. https://doi.org/10.1007/s10643-016-0825-7

Dixson, D. D., & Worrell, F. C. (2016). Formative and summative assessment in the classroom. *Theory into Practice, 55*(2), 153–59. https://doi.org/10.1080/00405841.2016.1148989

Dunn, K. E. (2016). Educational psychology's instructional challenge: Pre-service teacher concerns regarding classroom-level data-driven decision-making. *Psychology Learning & Teaching, 15*(1), 31–43. https://doi.org/10.1177%2F1475725716636975

Dunn, K. E., Airola, D. T., & Hayakawa, T. (2020). Pre-service teacher's efficacy, anxiety, and concerns about data and the new idea of anchored judgement. *Current Issues in Education, 21*(1), Article 1.

Ehri, L. C. (2020). The science of learning to read words: A case for systematic phonics instruction. *Reading Research Quarterly, 55*(1), 45–60. https://doi.org/10.1002/rrq.334

Efron, S. E., & Ravid, R. (2013). *Action research in education: A practical guide.* Guilford Press.

Every Student Succeeds Act of 2015, Pub. L. No. 114–95 114 § Stat. 117 (2015). https://www.congress.gov/114/plaws/publ95/PLAW-114publ95.pdf

Foley, E. A., Dozier, C. L., & Lessor, A. L. (2019). Comparison of components of the Good Behavior Game in a preschool classroom. *Journal of Applied Behavior Analysis, 52*(1), 84–104. https://doi.org/10.1002/jaba.506

Fox, J. J., & Gable, R. A. (2004). Functional behavioral assessment. In R. B. Rutherford, M. M. Quinn, & S. R. Mathur (Eds.), *Handbook of research in emotional and behavioral disorders.* The Guilford Press.

Freeman, J., Wilkinson, S., Kowitt, J., Kittelman, A., & Flannery, K. B. (2018). Research-supported practices for improving attendance in high schools: A review of the literature. *Educational Research and Evaluation, 24*(8), 481–503. https://doi.org/10.1080/138 03611.2019.1602546

Fuchs, L. S. (2004). The past, present, and future of curriculum-based measurement research. *School Psychology Review, 33*(2), 188–92.

Gill, P., Stewart, K., Treasure, E., & Chadwick, B. (2008). Methods of data collection in qualitative research: Interviews and focus groups. *British Dental Journal, 204,* 291–95.

Glanz, J. (1999). A primer on action research for the school administrator. *The Clearing House, 72*(5), 301–5. https://doi.org/10.1080/00098659909599413

Green, J. L., Schmitt-Wilson, S., Versland, T., Kelting-Gibson, L., & Nollmeyer, G. E. (2016). Teachers and data literacy: A blueprint for professional development to foster data driven decision making. *Journal of Continuing Education and Professional Development, 3*(1), 14–32.

Hester. P. P., Hendrickson, J. M., & Gable, R. A. (2009). Forty years later—The value of praise, ignoring, and rules for preschoolers at risk for behavior disorders. *Education and Treatment of Children, 32*(4), 513–35.

Howell, M., Dounavi, K., & Storey, C. (2019). To choose or not to choose?: A systematic literature review considering the effects of antecedent and consequence choice upon on-task and problem behavior. *Review Journal of Autism and Developmental Disorders, 6,* 63–84. https://doi.org/10.1007/s40489-018-00154-7

Hughes, J. N. (2003). Commentary: Participatory action research leads to sustainable school and community improvement. *School Psychology Review, 32*(1), 38–43. https://doi.org/10.1080/02796015.2003.12086179

Hulac, D. M., & Benson, N. (2010). The use of group contingencies for preventing and managing disruptive behaviors. *Intervention in School and Clinic, 45*(4), 257–62. https://doi.org/10.1177%2F1053451209353442

Individuals With Disabilities Education Improvement Act of 2004, P. L. No. 108–446, 20 U.S.C. (2004). https://ies.ed.gov/ncser/pdf/pl108-446.pdf

Jamshed, S. (2014). Qualitative research method-interviewing and observation. *Journal of Basic and Clinical Pharmacy, 5*(4), 87–88.

January, S. A., VanNorman, E. R., Christ, T. J., Ardoin, S. P., Eckert, T. L., & White, M. J. (2019). Evaluation of schedule frequency and density when monitoring progress with curriculum-based measurement. *School Psychology, 34*(1), 119–27. https://doi.org/10.1037/spq0000274

Jasper, A. D., & Taber-Doughty, T. (2015). Special educators and data recording: What's delayed recording got to do with it? *Focus on Autism and Other Developmental Disabilities, 30*(3), 143–53. https://doi.org/10.1177%2F1088357614547809

Johnson, R. B. & Onwuegbuzie, A. J. (2004). Mixed methods research: A research paradigm whose time has come. *Educational Researcher, 33*(7), 14–26. https://doi.org/10.3102%2F0013189X033007014

Johnston, M. (2005). The lamp and the mirror: Action research and self-studies in the social sciences. In K. Barton (Ed.). *Research methods in social studies education: Contemporary issues and perspectives* (pp. 40–48). Falmer Press.

Jones, T. L., Baxter, M. A. J., & Khanduja, V. (2013). A quick guide to survey research. *Annals of the Royal College of Surgeons of England, 95*(1), 5–7. https://doi.org/10.1308/003588413X13511609956372

Kelly, J., Sadeghieh, T., & Adeli, K. (2014). Peer review in scientific publications: Benefits, critiques, & a survival guide. *The Journal of the International Federation of Clinical Chemistry and Laboratory Medicine, 25*(3), 227–43.

Kim, K. (2016). Teaching to the data collection? (Un)intended consequences of online child assessment system, "Teaching Strategies GOLD." *Global Studies of Childhood, 6*(1), 98–112. https://doi.org/10.1177%2F2043610615627925

Lee, J., & Yoon, S. Y. (2017). The effects of repeated reading on reading fluency for students with reading disabilities: A meta-analysis. *Journal of Learning Disabilities, 50*(2), 213–24. https://doi.org/10.1177%2F0022219415605194

Lewis, T. J., Scott, T.M., Wehby, J. H., & Wills, H. P. (2014). Direct observation of teacher and student behavior in school settings: Trends, issues, and future directions. *Behavioral Disorders, 39*(4), 190–200.

Liew, J., Lench, H. C., Kao, G., Yeh, Y., & Kwak, O. (2014). Avoidance temperament and social-evaluative threat in college students' math performance: A mediation model of math and test anxiety. *Anxiety, Stress, & Coping, 27*(6), 650–61.

Lohmann, M. J., Boothe, K. A., Hathcote, A. R., & Turpin, A. (2018). Engaging graduate students in the online learning environment: A Universal Design for Learning (UDL) approach to teacher preparation. *Networks: An Online Journal for Teacher Research, 20*(2), Article 5.

Madden, N. A., & Slavin, R. E. (2017). Evaluations of technology-assisted small-group tutoring for struggling readers. *Reading & Writing Quarterly, 33*(4), 327–34. https://doi.org/10.1080/10573569.2016.1255577

Maggin, D. M., Cook, B. G., & Cook, L. (2018). Using single-case research designs to examine the effects of interventions in special education. *Learning Disabilities Research & Practice, 33*(4), 182–91.

Mandinach, E. B., & Gummer, E. S. (2013). A systemic view of implementing data literacy in educator preparation. *Educational Researcher, 42*(1), 30–37. https://doi.org/10.3102%2F0013189X12459803

Manfra, M. M. (2009). Action research: Exploring the theoretical divide between practical and critical approaches. *Journal of Curriculum and Instruction, 3*(1), 32–46.

Martinez-Mesa, J., Gonzalez-Chica, D. A., Bastos, J. L., Bonamigo, R. R., & Dunguia, R. P. (2014). Sample size: How many participants do I need in my research. *Anais Brasileiros de Dermatologia, 89*(4), 609–15.

Maxwell, J. A., & Loomis, D. M. (2003). Mixed methods design: An alternative approach. In A. Tashakkori & C. Teddie (Eds) *Handbook of mixed methods in social and behavioral research.* Sage Publications.

McGahie, W. C., Bordage, G., & Shea, J. A. (2011). Problem statement, conceptual framework, and research question. *Academic Medicine, 76*(9), 923–24.

McLeskey, J., Barringer, M-D., Billingsley, B., Brownell, M., Jackson, D., Kennedy, M., Lewis, T., Maheady, L., Rodriguez, J., Scheeler, M. C., Winn, J., & Ziegler, D. (2017). *High-leverage practices in special education.* Council for Exceptional Children & CEEDAR Center.

Moreno, G., & Bullock, L. M. (2011). Principles of positive behavior supports: Using the FBA as a problem-solving approach to address challenging behaviours beyond special populations. *Emotional and Behavioural Difficulties, 16*(2), 117–27. https://doi.org/10.1080/13632752.2011.569394

National Academy of Sciences, National Academy of Engineering, & Institute of Medicine Committee on Science, Engineering, and Public Policy. (2009). *On being a scientist: A guide to responsible conduct in research* (3rd ed.). National Academies Press.

National Research Council. (2000). *How people learn: Brain, mind, experience, and school.* National Academies Press.

Natow, R. S. (2019). The use of triangulation in qualitative studies employing elite interviews. *Qualitative Research, 20*(2), 160–73. https://doi.org/10.1177%2F1468794119830077

Newman, I., & Covrig, D. M. (2013). Building consistency between title, problem statement, purpose, & research questions to improve the quality of research plans and reports. *New Horizons in Adult Education & Human Resource Development, 25*(1), 70–79. https://doi.org/10.1002/nha.20009

Pew Research Center. (2021). *Questionnaire design.* https://www.pewresearch.org/methods/u-s-survey-research/questionnaire-design/

Piwowar, H. A., Becich, M. J., Bilofsky, H., & Crowley, R. S. (2008). Towards a data-sharing culture: Recommendations for leadership from academic health centers. *PLOS Medicine, 5*(9). https://doi.org/10.1371/journal.pmed.0050183

Poortman, C. L., & Schildkamp, K. (2016). Solving student achievement focused problems with a data use intervention for teachers. *Teaching and Teacher Education, 60,* 425–33. https://doi.org/10.1016/j.tate.2016.06.010

Ravid, R. (2020). *Practical statistics for educators* (6th ed). Rowman & Littlefield Publishers.

Reeves, A. A. (2011). *Where great teaching begins.* Association for Supervision and Curriculum Development.

Root, J., Saunders, A., Spooner, F., & Brosh, C. (2017). Teaching personal finance mathematical problem solving to individuals with moderate intellectual disabilities. *Career Development and Transition for Exceptional Individuals, 40*(1), 5–14. https://doi.org/10.1177%2F2165143416681288

Ruble, L. A., McGrew, J. H., Hang Wong, W., & Missall, K. N. (2018). Special education teachers' perceptions and intentions toward data collection. *Journal of Early Intervention, 40*(2), 177–91. https://doi.org/10.1177%2F1053815118771391

Russo-Campisi, J. (2017). Evidence-based practices in special education: Current assumptions and future considerations. *Child & Youth Care Forum, 46,* 193–205. https://doi.org/10.1007/s10566-017-9390-5

Sanders, S. (2019). *A brief guide to selecting and using pre-post assessments.* American Institutes for Research, The National Technical Assistance Center for the Education of Neglected or Delinquent Children and Youth.

Sheaffer, A. W., Majeika, C. E., Gilmour, A. F., & Wehby, J. H. (2021). Classroom behavior of students with or at risk of EBD: Student gender affects teacher ratings but not direct observations. *Behavioral Disorders, 46*(2), 96–107. https://doi.org/10.1177%2F0198742920911651

Scheithauer, M., Schebell, S. M., & Mevers, J. L, Martin, C. P., Noell, G., Suiter, K. C., & Call, N. A. (2020). A comparison of sources of baseline data for treatments of problem behavior following a functional analysis. *Journal of Applied Behavior Analysis, 53*(1), 102–20. https://doi.org/10.1002/jaba.549

Segool, N. K., Carlson, J. S., Goforth, A. N., von Der Embse, N., & Barterian, J. A. (2013). Heightened test anxiety among young children: Elementary school students' anxious responses to high-stakes testing. *Psychology in the Schools, 50*(5), 489–99.

Shavelson, R. J., & Stern, P. (1981). Research on teachers' pedagogical thoughts, judgments, decisions, and behavior. *Review of Educational Research, 51,* 455–98.

Simkins, S., & Allen, S. (2000). Pretesting students to improve teaching and learning. *International Advances in Economic Research, 6*(1), 100–12.

Szidon, K., & Franzone, E. (2009). *Task analysis*. National Professional Development Center on Autism Spectrum Disorders, Waisman Center, University of Wisconsin.

Taber-Doughty, T., & Jasper, A. D. (2012). Does latency in recording data make a difference? Confirming the accuracy of teachers' data. *Focus on Autism and Other Developmental Disabilities, 27*(3), 168–76. https://doi.org/10.1177%2F1088357612451121

Tashakkori, A., & Teddlie, C. (1998). *Mixed methodology: Combining qualitative and quantitative approaches*. Applied Social Research Methods Series (Vol. 46). Sage.

Toyama, Y., Heibert, E. H., & Pearson, P. D. (2017). An analysis of the text complexity of leveled passages in four popular classroom reading assessments. *Educational Assessment, 22*(3), 139–70. https://doi.org/10.1080/10627197.2017.1344091

Tuckman, B. W., & Harper, B. E. (2012). *Conducting educational research* (6th ed). Rowman & Littlefield Publishers.

United States Department of Education. (2011). *Information about the protection of human subjects in research supported by the Department of Education–Overview*. https://www2.ed.gov/policy/fund/guid/humansub/overview.html

United States Department of Health & Human Services. (2020). *Human subjects regulations decision charts: 2018 Requirements*. https://www.hhs.gov/ohrp/regulations-and-policy/decision-charts-2018/index.html

University of Oregon. (2021). DIBELS. https://dibels.uoregon.edu/

University of Oregon Center on Teaching and Learning. (2020). *Zones of Growth for DIBELS* (8th ed.) (Technical report 2001). https://dibels.amplify.com/docs/tech reports/Zog_tech_report_20200527.pdf

Venables, D. R. (2013). *How teachers can turn data into action*. ASCD.

Voit, E. O. (2019). Perspective: Dimensions of the scientific method. *PLoS Computational Biology, 15*(9), 1–14. https://doi.org/10.1371/journal.pcbi.1007279

Wayman, J. C., Jimerson, J. B., & Cho, V. (2012). *School Effectiveness and School Improvement, 23*(2), 159–78. https://doi.org/10.1080/09243453.2011.652124

Weijters, B., Cabooter, E., & Schillewaert, N. (2010). The effect of rating scale format on response styles: The number of response categories and response category labels. *International Journal of Research in Marketing, 27*(3), 236–47. http://doi.org/10.1016/j.ijresmar.2010.02.004

Whitcomb, S. A. (2018). *Behavioral, social, and emotional assessment of children and adolescents* (5th ed.). Routledge.

Wohlstetter, P., Datnow, A., & Park, V. (2008). Creating a system for data-driven decision-making: Applying the principal-agent framework. *School Effectiveness and School Improvement, 19*(3), 239–59. https://doi.org/10.1080/09243450802246376

Yell, M. L., Katsiyannis, A., & Bradley, M. R. (2017). The Individuals With Disabilities Education Act: The evolution of special education law. In J. M. Kauffman, D. P. Hallahan, & P. C. Pullen (Eds.). *Handbook of Special Education* (2nd ed.). Routledge.

Index

homework pass example, 49
hyperactivity, 120–21

IDEA. *See* Individuals with Disabilities Education Act
IEP. *See* Individual Education Program
implementation, of intervention, 64, *65, 66*; barriers to, *49*, 50, 53–54, *67*; by Mr. Bullock, 53, 54, *56–58*, 71–72, 102
implementation fidelity, 47, 49, 64, *65, 66*; common barriers to, *49*, 50, 53–54, *67*; resources for, *67*
Individual Education Program (IEP), 3–4, *4*, 27, *58*, 80; action research and, 103–6; individual meeting for, 81; sharing of research with team of, 87
individualized data, 106
Individuals with Disabilities Education Act (IDEA), 4, *5*, 38, 87, 103
informal data, 18
Institutional Review Board (IRB), 59–61, *60, 61*
instruction, systematic phonics, 112–13
intentionality, 54
intervention, 110; data collection in, *57*; implementation of, 64, *65, 66, 67*, 71–72, 79–80; materials financial cost of, *56*; next steps after, *55, 58*, 110–11, 113, 116–17; other job responsibilities and, 57; plan considerations for, *55, 56–58*, 58–59; plan design of, 47, *48*, 49, 110, 112–13, 115–16; planning for, *55*, 55–56; selection of, 103; taped problems, 86, 110
intervention-based solutions, 37–50
intervention materials, financial cost of, *57*
intervention success, evaluation of, *55, 57*, 71–72, 79–83, 87
interviews, *32*, 32–33; semi-structured, 32
introduction, of journal article, 95–96
IRB. *See* Institutional Review Board
IRB application: by Mr. Bullock, *61–63*; participant description in, *60, 63*
IRB form, sample, *61*
IRIS Center, 42–43

Jack (student), 114; data collection for, 113; evidence-based practices (EBPs) for, 112
Johnny (student), 35
journal article: discussion section of, 94–95; introduction of, 95–96

journals: academic, 39, 93; action research, 93, *94*; of education organizations, 41, 93–95
Julian (student), 104–5

letter, from Mr. Bullock, 86–87
library databases, 39
literature review, 95; sample of, *96–98*

Marvin (student), 121–22
Mary (student), 120
math delay, 124, *124*
mathematics exercise, Pierre and, 86
math facts, 29, *29*, 109–10
math teacher, in IEP meeting, 82
Matteo (student), 124, *124*
middle school, cheating in, 123

Nancy Drew (fictional character, *Nancy Drew* series), 72
The National Association of Special Education Teachers, 41
The National Research Council, 81
Newton, Isaac, 87–88
next steps, after intervention, *55, 58*, 110–11, 113, 116–17
numbers, quantitative research and, 8

observations, of behavior, 25, *26*
online courses, asynchronous, *92*
online office hours, *92*
Opal (student), 122
open-access education journals, 43, *44*, 45
open-ended questions, 28
Ophelia (student), 123–24
organizations, for educators, 41

paraprofessional training, 121
participant description, in IRB application, *60, 63*
peer-reviewed research, 38–39, 40, 43, 93–94
Penelope (student), 35
person responsible for actions in EBP, specification of, 64
Pierre (student), 109, 111; data collection for, 110; evidence-based practices for, 110; mathematics exercise and, 86
planning, for intervention, *55*, 55–56
population being researched, similarity to student of, 45–46
poster, use of bullet points in, 90

taped problems intervention, 86, 110
teachers: history, 80–82; math, 82; meetings with, 86; reflective practices of, 6; science, 81–82; special education, 81–82
test scores, anxiety and, 33
three-minute thesis project (3MT), 90; sample script for, *92*; videos of, 91, *91*
traditional research, action research *versus*, 6, *7*, 8
training, for paraprofessional, 121
transition goal, for high school student, 122
triangulation, of data, 33–34
Twitter: education discussions and, 38; student collaboration on, *92*

Universal Design for Learning (UDL), *90*
university database, evidence-based practices without, 41

unstructured interview, 32

verbal outbursts, 81–82
video presentation, 86
visuals, data presentation and, 88

webinar, 91
websites: for evidence-based practices, *43*; for special education EBPs, *43*
willingness, for implementation of intervention, 47
Wilson Reading training, 112–13
Wong (Mrs.), 112–14
work samples, 21, 22, *23*, *24*, 25
writing: disability, 123–24; of journal articles, 94–95
written notes, 86

Zoom, *92*

About the Author

∙∙

Marla J. Lohmann, PhD, is an associate professor of special education at Colorado Christian University, where she teaches courses on supporting students with disabilities, assistive technology, and action research. Dr. Lohmann has been in the field of education for over 20 years and is passionate about ensuring success for all children and their teachers. You can connect with her via Twitter: @MarlaLohmann.

Made in the USA
Monee, IL
28 April 2023